Contents

BIBLE STUDY GUIDE

What God Really Thinks About Women

SHARON JAYNES

HARVEST HOUSE PUBLISHERS

EUGENE, OREGON

Cover photo © iStockphoto / susabell

Cover by Garborg Design Works, Savage, Minnesota

WHAT GOD REALLY THINKS ABOUT WOMEN BIBLE STUDY GUIDE
Copyright © 2010 by Sharon Jaynes
Published by Harvest House Publishers
Eugene, Oregon 97402
www.harvesthousepublishers.com

ISBN 978-0-7369-3046-8

Printed in the United States of America

10 11 12 13 14 15 16 17 18 / BP-SK / 10 9 8 7 6 5 4 3 2 1

A New Day for Women

In the pages of *What God Really Thinks About Women*, we take a journey to look at the life of Jesus and His radical countercultural response to women during His 33 years of earthly ministry. We sit by the well with the Samaritan woman, expecting insult and rejection but receiving acceptance and love. We stand with the woman caught in adultery, expecting condemnation and death but finding forgiveness and a chance to start anew. We reach out our hand with the bleeding woman to touch the hem of Jesus' garment in secret, only to be healed and publicly affirmed. We rise from the ruins of life with Mary Magdalene and run with purpose to announce the miracle of Jesus' resurrection. But there is so much more to learn. My hope and prayer is that the words in *What God Really Thinks About Women* will merely whet your appetite to learn more about the deep, deep love God has for His female image bearers.

Jesus came to set the captive free. That freedom was extended to women who had been shackled by a culture that considered them less than men in every way. They were demeaned, disregarded, and devalued. In chapter 1 of *What God Really Thinks About Women*, we learn that by the time Jesus was born women were not allowed to eat with or talk to men in public, were not seen as trustworthy witnesses in a court of law, and were not allowed to study the Torah (the Scriptures) under a rabbi's teaching. A woman was considered a man's property—first her father's and then later her husband's. Women moved about as little gray shadows in the background of society, rarely seen and seldom heard.

But Jesus came to change all that. He ignored race, rank, and religious boundaries at every turn. He affirmed, validated, and honored women in God's family. Jesus spoke with, ministered to, and taught women just as readily as He did His male followers. "Just as surely as Jesus overturned the money changers' tables in the temple, He overturned the exploitation and mistreatment of women (Matthew 21:12; Mark 11:15; John 2:15). He overruled the tightly held views of a society that kept women hidden in the fabric of life and blending inconspicuously into the background."[1] Jesus pulled women from the shadows and set them center stage to play leading roles in God's redemptive plan.

This Bible study guide is not intended to be used without the prior reading of *What God Really Thinks About Women*. Much of the study builds on what we learn in those pages. Doing the study without reading the book would be like erecting walls of a building without pouring the foundation first. Each lesson coincides with the same numbered chapter title, and expands upon one or more aspect covered in the chapter. This study guide is for those who want to go deeper, learn more, and solidify their understanding of God's view of women.

I want to reiterate a point made in the book regarding the idea of knowing what God thinks about any subject, be it what He thinks about money, marriage, worship, prayer, sin, or any number of questions on how to live a godly life. During one of Philip's last conversations with Jesus, he asked, "Lord, show us the Father and that will be enough for us" (John 14:8).

Jesus answered, "Don't you know me, Philip, even after I have been among you such a long time? Anyone who has seen me has seen the Father. How can you say, 'Show us the Father'? Don't you believe that I am in the Father, and that the Father is in me? The words I say to you are not just my own. Rather, it is the Father, living in me, who is doing his work. Believe me when I say that I am in the Father and the Father is in me; or at least believe on the evidence of the miracles themselves" (verses 9-11).

The writer of the book of Hebrews tells us that Jesus is "the exact representation of [God's] being" (Hebrews 1:3). The original Greek word for "exact representation," *charakter*, describes the imprint of a die or the impression of a coin. For example, if you took a coin and pressed it into wax, you would have an exact representation. So when we see Jesus, we see God.

Can we really know what God thinks about women? I believe we can. We have only to look at the words and actions of His Son. Time and time again God affirmed His love for His daughters through Jesus. All through the New Testament we see that Jesus was on a mission to restore fallen humanity in every sense of the word. Part of that redemptive process involved setting women free from the cultural oppression that had them bound and kept them from fulfilling God's original intent as His female image bearers. Jesus came to restore women and their rightful place of dignity as one-half of a whole, as coheirs and coworkers with their male counterparts. His radical countercultural attitude toward women flew in the face of a patriarchal society that considered women less than men in all regards. He was a radical reformer who showed the world just what God thinks about women. I can hardly wait to open the pages of the Bible and delve in. Let's get started.

※

CREATED FOR DIVINE PURPOSE

Because we began our journey of discovering what God really thinks about women in the book of Genesis, let's begin our Bible study there as well. Here is a wonderful quote I'd like you to ponder: "In majestic strokes and with cosmic vistas, the first page of the Bible sets forth the story of God's dealings with humankind within the designs of creation. The beginnings of human history are correlated to the beginnings of time itself, and human life is described as the glorious culmination of God's creative endeavors."[1]

Now, open your Bible to Genesis 1.

1. Read through the chapter and note the verses where God said that what He created was "good." How many times do you discover those words?

2. How did God create everything up to verse 26?

3. Look closely at Genesis 1:26. What does it say about who created man?

Who do you think is included in the "Us?"

Read John 1:1-4 and note where Jesus was at creation.

4. How was the manner in which God created man different than the manner in which He created everything prior? (Genesis 1:27; 2:7, 2:7,21-22)

5. How was the nature of man different from all the other creatures God created? (Genesis 1:26)

6. We tend to use the word "man" to mean a male human being. However, in the Hebrew text of Genesis 1 the word "man" means "human" or "mankind." That is why Genesis 1:27 specifies that God created man, both male and female. How was this reiterated in Genesis 5:1-2?

7. Let's hop over to the New Testament for just a moment. Read Mark 8:31. How does Jesus refer to Himself?

Jesus refers to Himself as "Son of Man" 81 times in the Gospels. There are two Greek words that mean "man": *anthropos* and *aner*. While *aner* means "male," *anthropos* is the gender-inclusive word that means "human." In these words, Jesus was emphasizing that He was human. Of course, we know that Jesus was a male, but His emphasis here was His humanness.

8. Genesis 2 is a retelling of the creation account, focusing on the creation of man—both male and female. What did God say about the lone man in Genesis 2:18?

9. Did you notice that God didn't create woman right after He decided that it was "not good for the man to be alone"? What happened next? Read Genesis 1:19-20. What would Adam have felt after seeing all those animals walking two by two?

10. God often waits for us to realize our need before meeting our need. What do the following verses say about how God meets our needs?

Matthew 6:8

Ephesians 3:20

Philippians 4:19

11. Man had a need and God met it by creating "a helper." The Hebrew word is *ezer* and means "one who comes along to rescue." What did Eve rescue Adam from?

12. As mentioned in chapter 1 of *What God Really Thinks About Women*, this same word, *ezer,* is used of God as our helper, and it also refers to military protectors and allies. It is not a word that implies rank, but it does imply role. Look up the following verses and note how the words "help" and "helper" are used.

Exodus 18:4

Deuteronomy 33:7

Deuteronomy 33:26

Deuteronomy 33:29

Psalm 20:2

Psalm 33:20

Psalm 70:5

Psalm 89:19 (translated "strength" in the NIV)

Psalm 115:9-11

Psalm 121:1-2

Psalm 124:8

Psalm 146:5

Hosea 13:9

Now how do you feel about the fact that God created you, a woman, as a helper?

13. Read the following verses and note one of the most important ways you can be an *ezer*.

    Ephesians 6:10-18

14. After God created Eve, at the close of the sixth day, what did He say about all that He had made? (Genesis 1:31)

15. What was Adam and Eve's role in the garden? (Genesis 1:26, 28)

16. Were any job descriptions or gender-specific delegation of duties given for Adam and Eve?

17. The disobedience of Adam and Eve, often referred to as the "fall," was certainly the most tragic event in history. Read Genesis 3:13-19 and list the results of the fall for:

Man

Woman

The Serpent

(Note: Man, woman, and the serpent were judged, but only the serpent and the ground were cursed. God's words to Adam and Eve told of the inevitable consequences of their sin.)

18. Who did God say would eventually crush Satan's head? (Genesis 3:15)

The word "offspring" used here is the Hebrew word *zera* and means "seed." If you remember from *What God Really Thinks About Women*, the ancient Greeks believed that a man's seed contained tiny humans and a woman's only role in procreation was as the soil into which the seed was planted. However, in Genesis 3:15 God states that the offspring or seed of the woman would destroy the enemy. Scientists didn't discover that a woman had anything other than a passive role in procreation until 1827 when Carl Ernest von Baer discovered the human ovum and subsequently a woman's eggs. Isn't it exciting when science discovers what God has already told us?

Another thought on this verse. Genesis 3:15 (NKJV) was not clear on who the "seed" was, but the rest of the Bible answers that question. We know how the story ends. Who is the seed that eventually crushed the enemy's head?

Now tell me, does woman have a significant role in God's plan of redemption?

19. Some have said that woman was the cause for the fall of mankind. However, what do the following New Testament verses tell us?

Romans 5:12-19

1 Corinthians 15:21-22

Make no mistake, both Adam and Eve were present when the deed was done.

20. How did Adam and Eve's disobedience affect all mankind? (Romans 5:18-19)

21. What did Jesus come to do?

    Matthew 20:28

    John 10:10

    1 Corinthians 15:20-22

    Hebrews 2:14-15

    1 John 3:8

22. Sin, death, fear, shame, guilt, doubt, and spiritual death entered the world through Adam and Eve. No longer did men and women live free and unashamed. They were now living in a darkened world, held captive by the consequences of sin. But Jesus came to set us free and restore what we had lost.

What will ultimately set us free? (John 8:32)

Truth is not simply a way of thinking or speaking. Truth is a person. What did Jesus say about His identity? (John 14:6)

Combining these two verses, what works together to set us free?

23. Read and record Galatians 5:1. What does that mean to you?

24. Jesus would die tragically and rise triumphantly to restore what was lost by Adam and Eve's disobedience. What do the following verses tell us about our new life in Christ? (2 Corinthians 5:14-19, focusing on verse 17)

The *NIV Study Bible* notes: "Redemption is the restoration and fulfillment of God's purposes in creation, and this takes place in Christ, through whom all things were made and in whom all things are restored or created anew."[2]

25. As a new creation in Christ, our purpose is to glorify and enjoy God during our short time on earth. "When anything in creations fulfills its purpose, it brings glory to God."[3] How are you glorifying God with your life?

26. Let's end today's lesson by praising God with the words of Psalm 118:5. Look up the verse and make it your prayer of praise today.

What does God really think about women? Women are God's female image bearers—the grand finale of all creation! After God created woman, He looked on all that He had made, and it was "very good." After Adam and Eve's sin, God did not turn His back on mankind but set the plan of redemption in motion. Women were going to play a major role in that redemption plan.

Lesson 2

ℬLESSED 𝒯HROUGH ℛADICAL ᴼBEDIENCE

I f there is one lesson we can learn from Mary, the mother of Jesus, it is the amazing impact of a person's obedience to God's call on her life. In this lesson we will focus on the results of radical obedience.

1. As a building block for today's lesson, review Luke 1:26-45 and record Mary's response to Gabriel's message. (Luke 1:38)

Can you say that about yourself today?

2. What did Mary call herself in Luke 1:38?

The Greek word for "servant" that Mary used here is *doulos* or *doule* (the feminine form). It can also be translated "bondslave" or "bond-servant," and is defined as "one who gives himself up to the will of another, without any idea of bondage."[1]

When God gave the law to Israel, He established what was called a Sabbatical year. At the end of every seven years, the Israelites were commanded to forgive all their debts and free all their slaves. If a slave loved his master and did not want to leave, then he could choose to stay. As a symbol of his voluntary servitude, the servant placed his head against the master's door frame and the master pierced the servant's ear with an awl. By this act of being pierced, the freed servant was declaring that he or she was choosing to serve the master forever. To become a bondservant was the choice of the slave set free. In return, the master made a commitment to care for the bondservant for the rest of his or her life. Several New Testament writers referred to themselves as a *dulous*, or bondservant of Christ. (Titus 1:1; James 1:1; 2 Peter 1:1 NKJV)

> How does the Old Testament act of becoming a bondservant relate to the New Testament believer being a bondservant of Christ?

3. Read and record Elizabeth's summation of Mary's attitude toward God. (Luke 1:45)

Can you say that about yourself today?

4. Even though Gabriel described what was going to happen to Mary, I am sure she didn't completely understand how this miracle would take place. Are there circumstances in your own life where you know God is working, but you don't completely understand how the miracle could possibly take place? Explain.

5. Mary didn't understand completely, but she obeyed God totally. Why? Because she trusted Him.

   Read her song of praise recorded in Luke 1:46-55 and note what she knew about God's character and His ways.

6. Mary's song is very similar to Hannah's song of praise to God when she dedicated her son Samuel. Read her song of praise recorded in 1 Samuel 2:1-10 and note the similarities.

7. It is difficult, if not impossible, to put that amount of trust in a stranger. How does our level of knowledge of God relate to our level of trust in Him?

8. Let's look at how other people in the Bible responded to God's call on their lives. Match the person with his or her *initial* response to God.

Noah (Genesis 6:9-22)   Obeyed and sacrificed

Abraham (Genesis 12:1,4)   Questioned God's plan

Abraham (Genesis 22:1-12)   Interfered with God's plan

Sarah (Genesis 18:12)   Ran away from God

Rebekah (Genesis 27:5-10)   Obeyed and built

Moses (Exodus 3:11,13; 4:1)   Argued and asked for a sign

Gideon (Judges 6:11-19)   Obeyed and left

Jonah (Jonah 1:1-3)   Laughed at God's plan

9. The story of God testing Abraham in Genesis 22 can be difficult to read. However, it is a wonderful account of the blessings of radical obedience. What did God say to Abraham about the result of such obedience? (Genesis 22:15-18)

Read Hebrews 11:17-19. What was Abraham's assurance?

10. I believe one reason we don't obey God quickly is because, in our human minds, what He is asking doesn't make sense to us. Look at the following commands and put a check by the ones

that made little to no *human* sense. Forget hindsight. Pretend you don't know the outcome of each situation.

- God told Noah to build an ark when it had never rained on the earth before. The earth at that time had been watered by a mist that rose from the ground.[2] (Genesis 6:9-22)

- God told Abraham to leave his country and his family but did not tell him where he was going. (Genesis 12:1)

- God called Moses, an apparent stutterer, to be His spokesman. (Exodus 4:10-11)

- God told Joshua about His battle plan for defeating Jericho. The armed men and seven priests were to march around the walls of Jericho once a day for six days. Then on the seventh day, they were to march around seven times, blowing horns. On the final lap, the priests were to give a long blast and the fighting men were to shout. (Joshua 6:1-5)

- God called the cowardly Gideon (who was hiding in a winepress at the time) to lead the Israelite army. (Judges 6:11-16)

- God instructed Gideon to cut the number of soldiers going to battle against the Midianites from 32,000 to 300 (Judges 7:1-8). He then told them to blow trumpets and smash jars as the battle plan (Judges 7:17-21). (This is a great story!)

I don't know about you, but I checked them all. What does this tell you about God's ways and our ways? (Isaiah 55:8-9)

What would have happened in each of those situations if the person had not obeyed because the command made no sense to him?

11. After God freed the children of Israel from the slavery of the Egyptians, He sent them on a course to the Promised Land. Why was the first generation of freed Israelites *not* permitted to enter? (Numbers 14:21-23; Deuteronomy 9:23-24)

12. As long as the Israelites disobeyed God, they walked in circles in the desert. Yes, they were *saved* from the Egyptians, but they never experienced the *abundant life* that God had planned all along. But all that changed with the second generation. If the first generation was not allowed to enter because of unbelief and disobedience, why do you think the next generation was permitted in?

    What did they tell Joshua they were willing to do? (Joshua 1:16)

13. Now, dear friend, what do you need to do to enter your God-ordained promised land?

    What does your promised land look like? I don't know, but I do know it is good. What does 1 Corinthians 2:9 tell us about the plans God has for those who love Him?

14. Mary tells us how to practice radical obedience in John 2. What did she say to the servants after she realized the wine was about to run out? (John 2:5)

15. How do we know if what we are sensing is God's voice? Look up the following verses and note four checkpoints.

    Does it line up with God's Word? (Psalm 119:11,105,133,169)

    Does it line up with God's character? (Psalm 119:68)

    Does it line up with God's ways? (Psalm 25:10; 77:13)

    Does it require faith and dependence on God? (Hebrews 11:6)

16. Read Luke 5:1-10.

    What did Jesus tell Peter to do?

    What was Peter's initial response?

    Why did Peter obey?

What was the result of Peter's obedience?

What was Peter's response to Jesus' blessing?

Can you say that with Peter today? "Lord, I don't understand why you are telling me to do this, but _____ _____ _____ _____, I will do it."

Friend, if you wrote, "because You said so" in those blanks and then follow through with obedience, you will be blessed!

17. This wasn't the only time Jesus helped Peter bring in a miraculous catch. Read John 21:1-9. How long had Peter and John been fishing?

What had they caught in their own efforts?

What did they catch when they obeyed Jesus and threw their nets on the other side?

We can work our hardest in our own strength, but with little results. But when we listen to Jesus and obey His directives, He will show us where to cast the nets for an abundant catch!

18. Jesus is our ultimate example of radical obedience. Read the following verses and note His radical obedience to His Father.

    John 6:38

    John 8:28-29

    John 12:49-50

    John 17:4

19. Was obedience always easy for Jesus? Describe His anguish while praying in the Garden of Gethsemane. (Matthew 26:36-44)

20. What was the result of Jesus' radical obedience? (Romans 5:19)

21. Some say that they would obey God if they could hear Him audibly speak. Let's play this little game.

    When you were a child, did your parents speak to you audibly?

    Did you always obey what they said?

Why did you disobey them? Give three reasons.

How are those reasons similar to why we do not obey God?

Can you see any correlation between a child not obeying earthly parents and a believer not obeying his/her heavenly Father?

22. Every time we read God's words in the Bible, we have the opportunity to listen to Him. If we need to hear His words out loud, then we need only to read them out loud. How would your life be different if you made a decision to be radically obedient to God?

23. What does Ephesians 2:10 tell you about who you are?

What were you created to do?

When did God prepare the work He has for you to do?

If Mary were sitting beside you, I think she would say the same thing she said to the wine stewards in John 2:5. I know we've already recorded them, but let's do it again.

24. Now, let's bring it home. If you are willing to live a life of radical obedience to God, fill in the following blank with your name. Whatever God says, I, _____, will do.

If you have a New American Standard Bible, read John 2:5 in that translation as well. And if you wrote your name in that blank, hang on to your hat! God is about to take you to some amazing places!

What does God really think about women? He loves women so much that He has great plans for them and calls them to radical obedience in order to experience the abundant life. A woman is God's workmanship, created in Christ Jesus to do good works, which God prepared in advance for her to do.

COMMISSIONED TO GO AND TELL

Jesus came to free us all from the darkness that descended when sin and death entered the world in the Garden of Eden. But there is an enemy who does everything within his power to keep us from experiencing the abundantly blessed, spiritually free life God intended. This week we will look through the eyes of Mary Magdalene as Jesus brought her out of the darkness and into His light.

1. Read Luke 8:1-3. Who is mentioned as a part of Jesus' ministry team?

   How is Mary Magdalene described?

2. I remember being in Sunday school as a young teenager and hearing my teacher explain that demons were not real. "People didn't know what caused disease and sickness back then," she began, "so they blamed them on demons." Are demons real? Is the enemy, Satan, real? Let's take a look and see what the Bible has to say. Read the following verses and note: How did demons

affect their hosts? How did Jesus confront the demons? How did the demons respond to Jesus' commands?

Matthew 8:28-32

Matthew 9:32-33

Matthew 12:22

Matthew 17:14-18

Luke 4:31-41

3. Can you think of an incident in the Gospels where Jesus spoke to an illness? Can you think of any incident in Scripture when an illness spoke back to Jesus? What is the difference between the way Jesus approached healing someone with a physical illness and delivering someone from demons?

4. Demons thrive in darkness. What does light do to darkness? How did Jesus refer to Himself? (John 8:12)

5. How is God described in 1 John 1:5?

6. What do the following verses teach about the relationship of darkness and light on a spiritual level?

   John 1:6-9

   John 12:46

   Acts 26:15-18

   Ephesians 5:8

   Colossians 1:13-14

   1 Peter 2:9

7. Read John 10:10 and note what the enemy tries to do and what Jesus came to do.

8. One way the enemy still attacks women today is through lies. It is how he has always operated. It is his MO, so to speak. He tells women we aren't who God says we are and that we cannot do what God has planned for us to do. The lies tell us that we are less than what God has created us to be. That is why it is so important to know the truth. Let's look at how Jesus fought the lies of the enemy in the desert.

   Read Matthew 3:16-17. What had God just spoken about Jesus? List three aspects of God's announcement.

   Now read Matthew 4:1-11. How do the three temptations of Satan correlate to the three aspects of God's announcement at Jesus' baptism?

9. Jesus was hungry. How long had it been since He had eaten?

   The enemy knew Jesus was hungry, so that is the first area he attacked. The enemy is an opportunist and attacks us at our weakest point. What does it mean to be an opportunist?

   Read Luke's account of Jesus' temptation in the desert. What does he tell us in Luke 4:13?

10. Jesus' temptations were very real. What do Hebrews 2:17-18 and

4:15-16 tell us about how Jesus' temptations relate to our own personal struggles?

11. Although Jesus was the Son of God, He defeated Satan in the wilderness by using a weapon that every Christian has at his or her disposal. It is one weapon the enemy cannot resist. What is that weapon? (Ephesians 6:17)

How did Jesus begin each of His responses to Satan's temptations?

(For more on how to recognize the enemy's lies and replace them with truth, see my book *"I'm Not Good Enough"...and Other Lies Women Tell Themselves.*)

12. How does the knowledge that you have been delivered from darkness, empowered by the Holy Spirit, and equipped by the Word of God give you confidence to live in victory?

What does 1 John 4:4 tell you about the power that is within you?

13. Even though we may not have been delivered from seven demons the way our sister Mary Magdalene was, if we know Jesus as Savior and Lord, we have been delivered from the dominion

of darkness and brought into the light of Christ Jesus (Colossians 1:13). What does Jesus call believers? (Matthew 5:14)

14. Now that we have the light of Christ living in us, what does God call us to be in 2 Corinthians 5:20?

What is the purpose or role of an ambassador?

How are you an ambassador for Christ in your everyday life?

15. An ambassador represents a person or a country. What are Christians called in 1 Peter 2:11?

If you are an alien in this world, where is your citizenship? (Philippians 3:20)

16. Mary Magdalene is often called the "apostle to the apostles." Define the word "apostle." How is an apostle similar to an ambassador?

While Mary Magdalene was not one of the chosen 12, does she fit the description of an apostle?

Like Mary Magdalene, God saves us and then He sends us.

17. While the men fled the scene at Jesus' crucifixion, the women were there till the end. The least regarded by society were entrusted with their highest privilege of witnessing and relaying the most significant event in human history—the resurrection of Jesus Christ. Mary Magdalene was the first to witness the resurrection and the first commissioned to go and tell. In a culture where women were not allowed to testify in a court of law, Jesus appointed her as His key witness in the world's courtroom.

    What two directives did Jesus give Mary Magdalene in the garden? (John 20:17)

18. Did the disciples believe Mary Magdalene's testimony about Jesus resurrection? (Luke 24:11, Mark 16:11)

    Why do you think they did not believe her?

    How do you think they felt, knowing that Jesus appeared to her rather than to them?

    Does the fact that they did not believe Mary change the fact that she was chosen and commissioned by Jesus to tell the good news of His resurrection?

John 20:8 says that John "saw and believed." But we aren't told *what* he believed. It could be that he simply believed that the tomb was empty, as verse 9 notes that they still didn't understand that Jesus had to rise from the dead.

19. The prophet Samuel felt rejection when the people of Israel wanted to have a king rule over them rather than a prophet. What did God tell Samuel about the people's rejection? (1 Samuel 8:7)

    Did the fact that the people rejected God's messenger diminish the fact that he was called?

20. Dear friend, I hope you are catching a glimpse of a powerful truth. God still calls women out of the shadows to play leading roles in the redemption story. We should not be surprised if we face rejection. What does Isaiah prophesy about Jesus? Read Isaiah 53. Pay special attention to Isaiah 53:3.

21. If Jesus Himself experienced rejection, then we should not be surprised if we experience rejection as well. How did Jesus warn the disciples about future rejection? (Matthew 10:24-25)

    How did He tell them to face rejection in Matthew 10:26-31?

John Bunyan said, "If my life is fruitless, it doesn't matter who praises me, and if my life is fruitful, it doesn't matter who criticizes me." Once we know what God thinks of us, what others think of us matters very little.

22. What did Paul say about trying to please other people? (Galatians 1:10)

23. Mary Magdalene was allowed or invited to join Jesus' ministry team. How is this different from the man who was delivered from demons in the region of the Gerasenes? (Luke 8:38-39)

What does this tell you about God's plan for each of us? Are they the same?

24. As already mentioned, in Jesus' day women were considered unreliable witnesses and not even allowed to testify in court. However, God appointed them to be witnesses to two of most important events in history. Consider the following:

How did Luke know the intricate details of Mary's encounter with the angel Gabriel?

How did John know the intricate details of Mary Magdalene's encounter with Jesus at the empty tomb?

Look up and define the words "testimony" and "witness."

25. What did Jesus teach about the light we have been given? (Matthew 5:15-16)

How do we hide our light?

How do we shine our light?

26. Now, dear free friend, what are you going to do with the light you have been given?

27. "Mary Magdalene was a woman who had nothing to offer except the shattered pieces of her broken life."[1] God could have chosen anyone, and yet, He chose Mary Magdalene to be the first eyewitness to the resurrection of His Son and the first to herald the good news. What does that tell you about the kind of people God chooses to do great exploits for Him?

What does God think about women? He loves them so much that He made a way for them to be delivered from darkness and to live in the light of Christ. Not only that, God then entrusts His female image bearers to shine the light of Christ as ambassadors for God as if making His appeal through them.

Lesson 4

❧

LOVED AS GOD'S DAUGHTER

In the Old Testament, God has many names. He is Elohim, the Creator; El Elyon, God Most High; El Roi, the God Who Sees; El Shaddi, the All-Sufficient One; Adonai, the Lord; Jehovah, the Self-Existent One; Jehovah-Jireh, the Lord Will Provide; Jehovah-Rapha, the Lord Who Heals; Jehovah-Shalom, the Lord Is Peace; Jehovah-Raah, the Lord My Shepherd...and many more.

But in the New Testament, we are invited to call God by a new name. It is the name that Jesus referred to more than any other. That name is Father. J.I. Packer wrote, "For everything that Christ taught, everything that makes the New Testament new and better than the Old, everything that is distinctly Christian as opposed to merely Jewish, is summed up in the knowledge of the fatherhood of God."[1] Let's turn our attention to our heavenly Father who loves His girls.

1. What did Jesus call the woman who had been bleeding for 12 years? (Matthew 9:22)

How do you think those words made her feel?

How does it make you feel knowing that God looks at you as His daughter?

Jewish men were often called "sons of Abraham," but it was unheard of for a Jewish woman to be called a "daughter of Abraham." Once again, Jesus showed the world that women were just as valuable as men in the kingdom of God.

2. Read Matthew 6:6-9 and note how many times Jesus referred to God as Father.

3. Look up the following verses and note the references to God as our Father or you as His child.

   2 Corinthians 6:18

   Galatians 4:6-7 (Don't let it throw you that this verse talks about "sons." We're going to get to that in a moment.)

   1 John 3:1

4. Read Ephesians 1:4-6 and note how we were brought into the family of God.

"In ancient Rome, fathers chose a child for adoption when they were not able to have children of their own. They adopted a son in order to have someone to carry on the family name and inherit their property. It was a legal relationship: All ties to the child's natural family were severed, and the child was placed in a new family with the same prestige and privileges of a natural child, including becoming an heir. If the child had any debt, it was immediately cancelled. The adoption was a sealed process with many witnesses making it official."[2]

5. In modern times, most adoptions are of babies. However, in biblical times adoption usually took place after the child was older and had proved to be fit to carry on the family name in a worthy manner. Going back to Ephesians 1:4-6, when did God decide to adopt you?

What did you do to deserve being adopted as God's daughter? (Ephesians 2:8-9)

At what point was your adoption made final or legally binding? (Ephesians 1:13-14)

6. Go back up to the explanation of adoption in question 4. "If the child had any debt, it was immediately cancelled." How was our debt canceled? (1 Peter 3:18)

7. Now let's talk about the word "sons." The Hebrew word "son"

does not necessarily mean male offspring. In the Old Testament, the word *ben* can mean a male son or children of both genders, male or female. Remember from lesson 1, Genesis 1 says that God created man, meaning humans. Then the Word says, "Male and female he created them" (Genesis 1:27). The word "son" can mean the offspring of a human. It does not always mean a male child.

In the New Testament Greek, the word *huios* is translated "son." And like the Hebrew word *ben,* it can mean a male child or it can refer to offspring, both male and female.

The apostle Paul wrote to the Galatians, "You are all sons of God through faith in Christ Jesus, for all of you who were baptized in Christ have clothed yourselves with Christ. There is neither Jew nor Greek, slave nor free, male nor female, for you are all one in Christ Jesus" (Galatians 3:26-28). What does that teach us about Paul's use of the word "sons"?

8. Here's another wonderful aspect of being called a "son of God." In those days, only male offspring could inherit the father's wealth. But not so in God's family. What does Paul call us girls in Romans 8:16-17?

9. And here's more good news for you, God's daughter. You never have to worry about the stock market going down or the economy crashing to ruin your inheritance. What does the book of 1 Peter tell us about the safety of our inheritance as a child of God? (1 Peter 1:3-4)

10. Our Abba, Father, has already given us a taste of our inheritance that is to come. What do you learn about this "down payment" or "deposit" in Ephesians 1:13-14?

What are you doing with that part of your inheritance? Are you investing wisely?

11. You are constantly on your heavenly Father's mind. How does Isaiah 49:15-16 assure you of that truth?

12. Read and record David's prayer in Psalm 17:8.

The term "apple of your eye" refers to the pupil of the eye. The pupil is necessary for sight and must be protected. That is how God sees you! You are the apple of His eye, and He will protect you.

David also refers to God's protection—"hide me in the shadow of your wings." This was a common Hebrew metaphor for protection against oppression, as shade protects from the oppressive heat of the hot desert sun. What picture comes to mind when you think of hiding under the shadow of your heavenly Father's wings?

13. Read Psalm 145:8-20 and make a list of your heavenly Father's attributes. Which one means the most to you?

14. What can separate you from the love of God? (Romans 8:38-39)

15. Read and record Isaiah 54:10. What will never be shaken?

I love the words "unfailing love." The Hebrew word is *hesed* and often translated "loving-kindness," "steadfast love," "grace," "mercy," "faithfulness," "goodness," and "devotion." *Hesed* is used 240 times in the Old Treatment and is considered one of the most important words in the vocabulary of the Old Testament.[3] Why? Because God's unfailing love is one of the most important themes of the entire Bible. It is who He is and what He does.

16. Isaiah 54:10 also states that God has "compassion" on you. The Hebrew word for compassion is *racham,* which means "to soothe; to cherish; to love deeply like parents; to be compassionate, to be tender...the verb usually refers to a strong love which is rooted in some kind of natural bond, often from a superior one to an inferior one. [Here's the best part.] Small babies evoke this feeling."[4]

If you are a mother, what feelings came over you when you looked at your babies? (To be on the safe side, think of them when they were sleeping.)

That is the word *racham.* That is how God feels about you! And the good news is, God continues to feel that way about us even when we grow up.

17. After Jesus' resurrection, He told Mary Magdalene exactly what to say to the disciples. Look up John 20:17 and fill in the blanks.

    Jesus said, "Do not hold on to me, for I have not yet returned to the _____. Go instead to my _____ and tell them, 'I am returning to my _____ and your _____, to my God and your God.'"

    This is actually the only time Jesus called His disciples "brothers." However, He did make a statement about who His true brothers and sisters were. Who did Jesus include in his family? (Mark 3:35)

18. Like all good fathers, our heavenly Father does not give us everything we want. What would happen if we gave our children everything they wanted?

    The woman with the 12-year bleeding received her healing, but others in the Bible did not always get exactly what he or she wanted. Paul gave us an example of a seemingly unanswered prayer in his own life. Read 2 Corinthians 12:7-10 and note what he said about his thorn in the flesh, which God did not remove.

What did God's refusal to remove Paul's problem cause Paul to do?

What can we learn from Paul's experience and how he viewed his "thorn"?

19. Like all good fathers, our heavenly Father has dreams for His daughters. What does Jeremiah 29:11-12 tell you about God's plan for your life?

20. Part of God giving us a "future and a hope" is telling others about the hope that is within us.

After the woman with the issue of blood received her healing, Jesus would not allow her to slip away without telling the good news. What did He push her to do? (Luke 8:45-48)

Do you think that required courage? Why or why not?

What do you think was the outcome of her testimony about her healing?

Why was this so radical and important in a day when women were rarely seen or heard?

Why was this risky for her?

How does this relate to you telling others about what God has done for you?

21. Read Jeremiah 1:1-12 and answer the following questions.

When did God design His plan for Jeremiah's life? (Jeremiah 1:1-9)

Did Jeremiah readily jump at the chance to fulfill God's call on his life?

How did God respond to Jeremiah's lack of confidence?

Write down the words to the first sentence in Jeremiah 1:17.

22. Read the following verses and note what you learn about God's plans for His children.

Exodus 9:16

Psalm 40:5

1 Corinthians 2:9

23. In conclusion, let's end today's lesson by basking in the light of God's great love for His daughters. Look up the following verses and note what you learn about God's love for you.

Psalm 13:5-6

Psalm 36:5

Psalm 63:3-4

John 3:16

John 15:13

Romans 5:5,8

Ephesians 5:1

1 John 3:1

1 John 4:10

And, dear sister in Christ, daughter of Abraham, here is my prayer for you:

> For this reason I kneel before the Father, from whom his whole family in heaven and on earth derives its name. I pray that out of his glorious riches he may strengthen you with power through his Spirit in your inner being, so that Christ may dwell in your hearts through faith. And I pray that you, being rooted and established in love, may have power, together with all the saints, to grasp how wide and long and high and deep is the love of Christ, and to know this love that surpasses knowledge—that you may be filled to the measure of all the fullness of God.
>
> Now to him who is able to do immeasurably more than all we ask or imagine, according to his power that is at work within us, to him be glory in the church and in Christ Jesus throughout all generations, forever and ever! Amen (Ephesians 3:14-21).

What does God think about women? God loves women so much that He made them coheirs with Christ. He adopts any woman who believes in Jesus Christ as Lord and Savior into His family. God protects, provides for, and has great plans for His daughters.

❧

Valued in Jesus' Teaching

During Jesus' day, women moved about as little gray shadows that blended in with the background of society. But Jesus pulled them center stage in the drama of redemption and gave them leading roles in the most important scenes of history. In *What God Really Thinks About Women*, we sit roadside as Jesus interacted with several women in the New Testament. We see how Jesus highly valued women in a culture that valued women very little. Today, let's focus on how Jesus treated a woman caught in adultery who was used by the Pharisees as bait to try to trick Jesus.

1. As a review, read John 8:1-11. Who was conspicuously missing?

Would you say that Jesus spoke to the woman caught in adultery with compassion or contempt?

How was Jesus' treatment toward this woman vastly different from that of the Pharisees'?

2. One way Jesus showed that He valued women was in His teachings on sexual sin and marriage. As we see in the story of the woman caught in adultery, there was a double standard when it came to sexual sin. Women were considered seductive and usually blamed for men's lusts and adulterous relationships.[1] Read Matthew 5:28-29 and note what Jesus said about sexual sin. Also note where He placed the blame.

How did this teaching go against the cultural norms?

How was Jesus protecting women and removing the double standard?

On whom was Jesus placing responsibility for lust?

3. Women were also devalued in the ease with which a man could divorce his wife. "A man only had to clap his hands three times to legally divorce his wife for something as trivial as burning the bread."[2] However, Jesus spoke against this practice that devalued women. Read Matthew 19:1-9 and note what Jesus said about divorce.

While this sounds logical to us in the twenty-first century, what was the disciples' response to Jesus' statement about divorce? (Matthew 19:10)

This was the disciples' response, mind you, not the Pharisees'. Here's how Eugene Peterson paraphrases their response in *The Message:* "If those are the terms of marriage, we're stuck. Why get married?"

Again, how did Jesus' teaching on divorce protect and value women?

4. What do you see added to Jesus' response to the Pharisees' question in Mark 10:2? (See Mark 10:3-9)

In those days, only a man could divorce his wife, not vice versa. How did Jesus' response go against the grain of the culture, level the playing field, and break down the walls of the double standard?

5. Later, Paul would write some revolutionary ideas for marriage. Read 1 Corinthians 7:1-5. How do these verses contrast with the commonly accepted belief of their day that women were the property of their husbands?

Paul uses the words "in the same way" in 1 Corinthians 7:4. What would that have meant to a wife of those days who had previously had literally no rights in a marriage?

6. As mentioned in chapter 1 of *What God Really Thinks About Women,* women in ancient Greece were considered a husband's property and were treated as such. Read Ephesians 5:25-33 and note Paul's teaching on how a husband should treat his wife.

How are men to love their wives?

How did Christ show love toward the church?

How was this radically different from the culture of Jesus' day that viewed women as a commodity?

7. This would be a good time to take a look at how Jesus valued women in every aspect of His teaching. Let's take a general look at more ways He highly valued women in a culture that valued women very little.

Luke mentions women in his Gospel more often than Matthew, Mark, or John. He showed how Jesus treated women with worth and dignity by referring to them in His parables and highlighting their actions as godly examples to emulate.

Jesus not only crossed gender boundaries to teach women, He also clarified His teaching with incidents from women's lives as He taught others. Look at the following parables and note if Jesus used a male or female as the main character. Give each parable a title. I'll get you started.

Luke 13:18-19 A *man* who planted a mustard seed.

Luke 13:20-21 A *woman* who

Luke 15:1-7

Luke 15:8-10

Luke 18:1-8

Luke 18:10-14

8. In a culture that devalued and ignored women, what was Jesus teaching by example as He referred to both women and men in His teachings?

9. Luke also showed an alternating pattern of Jesus healing men and women with similar ailments. Look up the following and notice the male/female healings and the similarities of their conditions.

Luke 6:6-11 and 13:10-17

Luke 7:11-16 and 8:40-42,51-56

Luke 8:1-2 and 8:26-38

Luke 5:12-16 and 8:40-48

What does this show you about Jesus' countercultural attitude toward the value of women?

10. Even before Jesus began His teachings and miracles, we see another pairing of a man and a woman. Who prophesied over the baby Jesus in the temple? (Luke 2:25-38)

Even at the very beginning of Jesus' life, we see that God is doing something new.

11. Read Luke 12:6-7. In a culture that placed little value on women, how do you think these words made the female listeners feel?

Here's how Eugene Peterson paraphrases Luke 12:6-7 in *The Message:* "What's the price of two or three pet canaries? Some loose change, right? But God never overlooks a single one. And he pays even greater attention to you, down to the last detail—even numbering the hairs of your head! So don't be intimidated...you're worth more than a million canaries."

12. The Gospels had a series of "firsts" that involved women. For example, for the first time women were listed in the genealogies. In Matthew 1, we read of the lineage of Jesus through Mary's line. It was unheard of for women to be listed in a genealogy, but when we turn from Malachi to Matthew, as God breaks His 400-year silence, we see that He is up to something new. Right away we sense that God is calling His female image bearers to take center stage. Let's take a look at these four women and see how God chooses whom He uses. Read Matthew 1:1-6 and note the four women who were listed other than Mary.

13. Scan the following verses and give a one-sentence description of each woman listed in Jesus' lineage.

Tamar (Genesis 38)

Rahab (Joshua 2)

Ruth (Ruth 1)

Bathsheba (her name isn't actually listed, but how is she described—2 Samuel 11:1-5)

Three of the four women had sordid pasts, and the other was from a cursed people. This should give each of us hope that no matter how bad our past has been, God is able to save us, redeem us, and use us for His glory! How does knowing how God used these four women in His redemptive plan give you hope?

The Scarlet Letter, a book written by Nathaniel Hawthorne, is the story of a young woman named Hester Prynne and her daughter. After the unmarried Hester became pregnant, she was forced to wear the letter *A* on her clothing at all times. Both mother and child were shunned by the community, and yet the father of the child remained a mystery.

I am so glad God chose these particular women to be listed in the lineage of Jesus. No letter *A* for these gals. Just the letter *R* for redeemed. God not only redeemed them from their pasts, but He then used them for kingdom purposes.

14. Now, let's go back to our sister standing before Jesus, expecting condemnation but receiving grace and forgiveness. Read the following verses and note what you learn about God's forgiveness.

    Ephesians 4:32

    Colossians 2:13-14 (According to these verses, what did God do to the charges against you?)

    Colossians 3:13

15. Did the woman caught in adultery have to do anything to earn her forgiveness?

    What does Ephesians 2:8-9 tell us about how we have received forgiveness and salvation?

This is one way that a relationship with Jesus differs from a religion. "Religion says you do what is right in order to earn acceptance, love and forgiveness. A relationship with God through Jesus Christ is not based on our performance because we already are accepted, loved and forgiven."[3]

16. Read the following and note what happens once you ask God to forgive you.

    Hebrews 10:17

    2 Corinthians 5:17

    1 John 1:9

17. What is God's final verdict for the repentant Christian? (Romans 8:1)

Receiving grace and forgiveness for the wrongs we have committed

is an act of faith. "It is difficult to fathom such extravagant unconditional love, yet so many of us leave His gift unopened. We admire
its wrapping or marvel at its enormity, but avoid getting too close.
Something within us cannot grasp the idea that God meant this for
us, so we put conditions on accepting His gift."[4]

We all have regrets—just different ones. The Bible says, "All have
sinned and fall short of the glory of God" (Romans 3:23). God is
offering you the same forgiveness He offered the woman caught in
adultery. Have you accepted that forgiveness?

What does God really think about women? God loves women,
and we can see that through the life of His Son.
Jesus showed a woman's great worth by including them in
His message and miracles. He reversed cultural practices that
exploited women and reinstated God's original design that
protected them against misuse and abuse. He called them
center stage to play leading roles in His plan of redemption.

❦

RESTORED THROUGH JESUS' MINISTRY

Every woman we meet in *What God Really Thinks About Women* was changed by Jesus. Some were healed, some were forgiven, some were delivered, and some were freed. But not one woman remained the same as she was before her life intersected with Jesus. He changed empty to full, rejected to accepted, and broken to whole. Let's take a seat by the well and listen in on Jesus' conversation with the Samaritan woman He came to save.

Empty to Full

1. Read John 4:1-42. The Samaritan woman we meet here is as empty as the water pot she carried on her head. What about her conversation with Jesus hints at the emptiness she felt in her heart?

   What about the time of day she came to the well lets you know she avoided women in the town?

2. Look up the definition of "empty" in the dictionary and note its meaning.

3. Has there ever been a time in your life when you felt empty? How did you try to fill that emptiness?

   What was the result of your efforts?

4. Consider this quote by Adrianne Gambucci: "Emptiness is a gift that opens us further to the transforming power of God." What do you think Gambucci meant by that?

5. What did Jesus offer the empty Samaritan woman at the well? (John 4:10)

   How did He describe this living water? (John 4:13-14)

6. This was not the only time Jesus talked about living water. Just six months before His crucifixion, on an eventful October day in Jerusalem, Jesus gave a similar invitation. It was the annual Feast of Tabernacles. Author Max Lucado paints the scene for us: "People had packed the streets for the annual reenactment

of the rock-giving water miracle of Moses. In honor of their nomadic ancestors, they slept in tents. In tribute to the desert stream, they poured out water. Each morning a priest filled a golden pitcher with water from the Gihon spring and carried it down a people-lined path to the temple. Announced by trumpets, the priest encircled the altar with libation of liquid. He did this every day, once a day, for seven days. Then on the last day, the great day, the priest gave the altar a Jericho loop—seven circles—dousing it with seven vessels of water."[1]

Perhaps it was at that very moment when Jesus stood up and commanded the crowd's attention. Read John 7:37-39 and record Jesus' words.

Teachers usually sat down to teach, but in this case Jesus stood up. This was important.

What does John tell us about the volume in which Jesus spoke?

One translation said Jesus "shouted" (NLT). Another said He "cried out" (NKJV). He wanted to make sure everyone heard the invitation.

How did the crowd respond to Jesus' words? (John 7:40-44)

Is this any different from those who hear Jesus' words today?

One more observation. To whom was Jesus speaking?

Were these religious folks who had come to celebrate a religious holiday, or was this a gathering of prostitutes, murderers, and thieves?

In the middle of a religious holiday celebration, Jesus stood and shouted that the people there were looking for thirst-quenching satisfaction in all the wrong places. It is only through a relationship with Him that they would find springs of living water to satisfy their souls. Religious activities might abate spiritual thirst for a short time, but only through a personal, ongoing relationship with Jesus Christ and the infilling of the Holy Spirit will that thirst be quenched permanently.

7. Jesus offered to fill the empty woman at the well with living water. He offers that same living water to anyone who will receive it. Read Revelation 22:17. What are the Spirit and the bride urging all to do?

8. Blaise Pascal once said, "There is a God-shaped vacuum in the heart of every man which cannot be filled by any created thing, but only by God, the Creator, made known through Jesus." How has this proved true in your own life?

Rejected to Accepted

9. Feelings of rejection often come from empty, lonely lives. Because of death, divorce, and deferred marriage, an estimated 31 million Americans live alone.[2] Many of the women we meet in

What God Really Thinks About Women struggle with feelings of rejection. Note how the following women might have felt rejection.

Mary of Nazareth

Mary Magdalene

The woman with the 12-year bleeding

The woman caught in adultery

The Samaritan woman at the well

10. Look up the definition of "rejection" in a dictionary and note its meaning.

11. What does the Bible teach about God's unconditional acceptance?

Romans 5:8

1 John 4:10,19 (Who loved first?)

12. Let's consider the follow quote by Mark Rutland in his book, *Streams of Mercy*. "Jesus stands behind the communion table with His nail-scarred hands outstretched and the light of mercy in His eyes. His voice, His words meet us with healing warmth as we drag our water-logged burdens up the rocky shoreline from life's most chilling seas. 'I love you,' He whispers. 'I forgive you. Come and dine.'"[3]

    What picture does that paint in your mind about God's acceptance?

13. Not only have we been totally and completely accepted by God, we have been pursued by Him. In our eyes we may see ourselves as pleading with God to accept us. The truth is, Jesus is standing at the door knocking, longing to come in. Read and record Revelation 3:20.

14. As a review, read and record John 4:4.

    God was pursuing this woman, and He sent His Son on special assignment. He does the same for you! How does the idea that God pursues a relationship with you make you feel about your value and worth?

15. What was the first question asked in the Bible? (Genesis 3:9)

What does that show you about God's desire to have a relationship with His children?

16. Not only are you accepted and pursued by God, you are chosen! Read the following verses about how God chose you.

    John 15:16

    Ephesians 1:4-6

    2 Thessalonians 2:13

17. Before we start feeling proud about being chosen by God, read 1 Corinthians 1:27-31 and note what kind of people God chooses.

    Why does God choose the weak?

    What does Paul say about his weaknesses? (2 Corinthians 12:7-10)

Broken to Whole

18. The Samaritan woman we meet at the well was no doubt broken by her circumstances and her inability to make life work on her own. Many of the women we meet in *What God Really Thinks About Women* were broken people—broken women whom Jesus made whole. I think one of the ways we can better picture what brokenness looks like is to think of ourselves as vessels created by God. Read Jeremiah 18:3-4.

    Who is the Potter?

    Who is the clay?

    How did the Potter decide what to form the clay into?

19. Read the following verses and note what you learn about the relationship between the Potter and the clay.

    Deuteronomy 32:6

    Psalm 119:73

    Psalm 139:13

    Isaiah 44:2

Isaiah 64:8

20. Read and record David's prayer in Psalm 138:8.

In *The Message*, Eugene Peterson says it this way: "Finish what you started in me, God. Your love is eternal—don't quit on me now." I love that! And you know what? God will not quit on you now—or forever.

21. What did Paul tell the Philippians about God's ability to complete what He had begun in them? (Philippians 1:6)

22. Now that we know God formed us, let's consider what happens when our particular pottery gets chipped, cracked, or broken.

Look up the definition of "broken" and note its meaning.

How did David feel about his life at the time he wrote Psalm 31:12?

What do you think he meant by that?

23. Let's consider the following quote by Meister Eckhart in *The Spirituality of the Imperfection*, written almost 700 years ago:

"Imperfection is the crack in the armor, the 'wound' that lets God in."

Paraphrase that in your own words.

Do you feel broken in any area of your life: physically, spiritually, or emotionally?

What did Jesus come to do? (Isaiah 61:1-3—Jesus read part of this in the synagogue at Nazareth, recorded in Luke 4:18-19.)

24. Jesus said, "Blessed are the poor in spirit, for theirs is the kingdom of heaven" (Matthew 5:3). There are two words Jesus could have used for the word "poor." The first one describes a person who lives just below the poverty line and has to scrape just to get by. The second, which is the one Jesus chose, means beggar—a person who is absolutely destitute. This person has no hope unless someone comes along and rescues her. What is Jesus saying about a person who is broken and spiritually bankrupt?

When someone is absolutely destitute, they know that there is no hope unless God reaches out and saves them. That is a person who will be truly blessed or as the word actually means, happy.

In *Brokenness: The Heart God Revives*, Nancy Leigh DeMoss describes brokenness as "the shattering of my self-will—the absolute surrender of my will to the will of God. It is saying 'Yes, Lord!'—no resistance, no chafing, no stubbornness—simply submitting myself to His direction and will in my life."[4]

25. Samuel Chadwick said, "It is a wonder what God can do with a broken heart, if He gets all the pieces." How did Jesus take the broken pieces of the following women's lives and make them whole?

Mary Magdalene

The woman with the 12-year hemorrhage

The woman caught in adultery

The Samaritan woman at the well

26. As we have looked at what it means to be broken, let me tell you what brokenness is not.

- Brokenness is not about being sad and gloomy.

- Brokenness is not about just crying and feeling sorry.

- Brokenness is not about being wounded by someone's actions or words.

- Brokenness is not about experiencing a tragedy in your life.

Now, all those things can lead to brokenness, but they do not define it. Brokenness is a matter of the heart. It is a giving up of our control and handing the reins to God. It is saying, "I can't do this on my own," and then trusting God to take complete control. That's why the poor in spirit can be happy.

Jesus came to bind up the brokenhearted. But that's not all. He takes the broken pieces of our lives and makes a beautiful mosaic—something more beautiful than we could ever have imagined. Jesus fills our empty spaces and moves into our hollow places.

What does God really think about women? God loves women so much that He sent His Son to seek out the empty and fill them to overflowing, to put His arms around the rejected and draw them in, and to bind up the brokenhearted and make them whole. Through His ministry, Jesus restored women spiritually, emotionally, and physically.

WELCOMED INTO GOD'S PRESENCE

As we discovered in *What God Really Thinks About Women,* Herod's Temple was built overlooking the city of Jerusalem. The temple was built by Herod and his sons between 19 BC–64 AD to appease the Jews. The original temple built by Solomon was small in comparison to the pagan temples of Herod's day. So when Herod built the temple, he wanted to make it "bigger and better."

Surrounding the temple proper was a series of concentric courts, each with increasing holiness as one proceeded closer to the Holy of Holies. The courtyards and ascending steps that led up to the Holy of Holies were enormous. The first, or lowest, courtyard was called the court of the Gentiles, and was open to Jews and God-fearing Gentiles. The second courtyard, one level up, was called the court of women, and only Jewish men and women could enter. That's as far as women could go. The other levels were only open to men. The entire setup was to separate people groups according to the prejudices of the day.

How did God feel about those man-made separations? Let's find out. Join me now as we walk into a roomful of men with a sinful woman who came to worship Jesus.

1. Read Luke 7:36-50. How is the woman with the alabaster jar described?

   Would she have been welcomed in such a gathering? Why or why not?

   What was Jesus' reaction to her display of worship?

   What was her attitude? Was she humble or prideful?

   What was Simon's attitude? Was he humble or prideful?

   Which person reflects your attitude the most?

   Did Jesus welcome her worship or turn her away?

2. Read the parable of the tax collector and the Pharisee in Luke 18:9-14. What similarities do you see between these scenarios?

3. In our last lesson, we looked at what it means to be broken. No doubt the sinful woman who anointed Jesus with perfume fit that description. Generally, broken people are more concerned

with what God thinks than with what people think. They tend to be open and transparent because they have nothing to lose. How did the woman who anointed Jesus' feet show that she cared more about what God thought than what people thought?

Would you say that you care more about what God thinks of you than what other people think of you? (Wow, that's a tough one, isn't it.)

4. What are some reasons you think men and women are reluctant to show outward displays of worship?

5. One stumbling block to showing outward displays of worship is pride. How did Simon's thoughts reveal his prideful attitude?

Read the following verses and note what God really thinks about pride.

Proverbs 3:34

Proverbs 16:5

Proverbs 18:12

Luke 1:50-52

James 4:6

6. How does Jesus' encounter with the woman who anointed Him paint a beautiful picture of James 4:10?

7. What does the Bible tell us about praising God for who He is and thanking Him for what He does?

1 Chronicles 16:8-10

1 Chronicles 16:34

Psalm 30:11-12

Psalm 100:4-5

Psalm 107:1,8

8. What did the writer of the letter to the Romans note as one of

the reasons for God's wrath? What did the people fail to do? (Romans 1:21)

9. The five levels that led up to the Holy of Holies in Herod's Temple were not God's original design. The original tabernacle consisted of an outer court for all to enter, an inner court (or Holy Place) for the appointed Levite priests, and the Holy of Holies, where the Ark of the Covenant was kept.

   What separated the Holy of Holies from the rest of the tabernacle? (Exodus 26:33)

10. The high priest only went into the Holy of Holies once a year. What he had to go through to prepare for going into the Holy of Holies is mind boggling (Leviticus 16). Let's just look at one aspect. Read Exodus 28:31-35. What was sewn around the hem of the high priest's robe?

   What was the purpose of the bells?

It was a frightening experience to go beyond the veil and enter the Holy of Holies. The priests would tie a rope around the high priest's ankle. As he entered, they would listen for the bells to know that God had not killed him. If they did not hear the bells, they knew God was not pleased and the high priest was dead. Then they would pull him out by the rope tied to his ankle.

Do you think the high priest entered the presence of God with confidence or with fear and trepidation?

11. Read Matthew 27:51-53 and answer the following questions. Much of Herod's Temple was different from the original tabernacle, but it still had the Holy of Holies.

Describe what happened in the temple when Jesus died?

How was the curtain (veil) torn?

Who do you think tore it?

12. What is the significance of the veil separating sinful mankind from God being torn? (Hebrews 10:19-22)

13. In the temple, there was a partition separating the Jews from the Gentiles, and another one that separated the Jewish women from the Jewish men. What did Paul say Jesus did to that physical wall that represented a spiritual separation of Jew and Gentile? (Ephesians 2:13-18)

14. Now who can enter God's presence and with what attitude? (Hebrews 4:15-16; 10:19-22)

Why can we enter God's presence with confidence?

15. In the Old Testament, priests had to continually offer sacrifices for their sins and the sins of the people. The high priests had to offer these sacrifices before they could enter the Holy of Holies (God's presence). Why don't we have to do that any longer?

Hebrews 7:23-27

Hebrews 9:24-26

Hebrews 10:10

When the veil was torn, in one sweeping motion God leveled the steps, removed the partitions, and granted equal access to His presence to all who believe! But we still have to choose to enter in.

16. Not only does God *welcome* us into His presence, He wants us to *remain* in His presence. What does that mean? Let's take a look at some of the last words Jesus spoke to the disciples before He went to the cross. After Jesus celebrated His last Passover dinner with the disciples, they left the upper room and headed for the Garden of Gethsemane. As they passed by ancient vineyards,

Jesus taught them what it means to abide in Him. Read John 15:1-17 and answer the following questions.

Who is the Gardener?

Who is the Vine?

Who are the branches?

What happens when a branch does not remain attached to the vine?

Why does that happen?

What was Jesus' answer to maintaining a flourishing Christian life?

The NIV uses the word "remain," which can also mean "abide." Both words are translated from the Greek word *meno* and mean to stay closely connected, to settle in for the long term. Abiding isn't about how much you know about God, but how well you know God. What do you see as the difference between the two? How can you know a lot about someone but not know them personally?

17. What are some ways we stay connected to the Vine?

A common phrase used today in regard to relationships is "connected." We say, "Let's go to lunch and connect." A friend moves to another state and we say, "Let's stay connected." A relationship grows cold and we say, "I don't feel connected to you any longer." In earthly terms, how do we stay connected with others? Give some practical examples.

How are those ways similar to the ways we stay connected with God?

18. According to Jesus' words recorded in John 15:1-17, what is the natural by-product or result of remaining or abiding in Him?

Fruit can mean various things in the Bible. Look up the following verses and note what you learn about:

Actions (Matthew 7:15-20)

Fruit of the Spirit (Galatians 5:22-23)

Good works (Titus 3:14)

19. What can we accomplish apart from Jesus? Read John 15:15. What is the difference between being busy for God and producing fruit that will remain?

20. Why does Jesus want us to abide in Him? Read and record John 15:9.

I want us to really get this. While Jesus talked about remaining in Him and bearing fruit, the main point is how much He loves us. Jesus longs for us to abide in Him because He wants to spend time with us! He cherishes the times you spend with Him. He loves you that much!

21. Finally, what is the ultimate response that will bubble up inside us when we remain in Christ and live a life of obedience to Him? (John 15:11)

22. Just as Jesus welcomed the woman with the alabaster jar into His presence, God welcomes us into His. Close out today's lesson by writing a note of thanks to God for loving you enough to make that possible.

*What does God really think about women? He welcomes
us into His presence, yes, but it is more than that. God
created us to be in relationship with Him and longs for us
to come into His presence. He wants to spend time with us!*

𝒪NVITED INTO 𝒥ESUS' 𝒞LASSROOM

During the time of Jesus, most rabbis thought it was inappropriate to teach women. While men were expected to attend synagogue and study the Torah, women were not. A common belief was that men learn, but women merely listen. They were treated as unteachable creatures. However, Jesus taught where women could hear, and He even commended women who crossed cultural and gender boundaries to learn Scripture. Let's spend this lesson exploring why it is so important for a woman to know God and His Word.

1. Read Genesis 3:1-3. What was Eve's core problem? Did she know the truth?

2. What can happen when we do not know God's truth? (Ephesians 4:14-15)

3. What did Moses pray in Exodus 33:13?

The Hebrew word for "know," which is used here, is a relational word. It is the same word that is translated "know" in the King James Version that says Adam *knew* Eve and she conceived a son. It is more than head knowledge. It is a knowing that leads to a relationship between God and the learner. It is "the meeting and marriage between ourselves and God...the highest and holiest happiest hope of the human heart, the thing we were all born hungering for, hunting for, longing for."[1]

> This is too good to pass up. What was God's reply to Moses' request? (Exodus 33:17)

Friend, that is His reply to your hunger to know Him as well.

4. In the Old Testament, women were expected to be present at the reading of the Torah (Scriptures). Read the following and note Moses' command.

Deuteronomy 31:9-13

Nehemiah 8:1-3

Somewhere in the 400 years that spanned the Old Testament and the New Testament, women were shunned from the classroom. The

layout of Herod's Temple reinforced what the religious leaders believed: Some people were more worthy of closer access to God than others.

5. It is difficult, if not impossible, to trust someone you do not know. It is difficult to have faith in someone who is only an acquaintance. Faith requires a steady diet of the truth to remain strong. What did David say is one benefit of knowing God? (Psalm 9:10)

6. What did the psalmist long for?

Psalm 119:12

Psalm 119:18

Psalm 119:97

Psalm 119:103

Psalm 119:105

7. What did the psalmist know about God?

Psalm 20:6

Psalm 25:10

Psalm 100:3

Psalm 119:68

Psalm 119:75-76

8. Part of knowing God involves understanding His character and His ways. How would you like to see a job description for God? While our finite minds cannot comprehend God's infinite role, He gives us a tiny glimpse in the book of Job as He replies to Job's many questions regarding the tragedy of his life. Read Job 38–41 and note what you learn about God. You may want to spread this assignment out over a few days and savor God's description of Himself.

9. Consider the following quote: "We must learn to take ourselves in hand, address ourselves, preach to ourselves, remind ourselves of who God is, what God has done, and what God has pledged Himself to do."[2]

How would such reminders of what God has done and has promised to do buoy our faith and trust in Him?

10. As we mentioned in the introduction, one way we know God is through the life of His Son. John wrote, "We know also that the Son of God has come and has given us understanding, so that we may know him who is true. And we are in him who is

true—even in his Son Jesus Christ. He is the true God and eternal life" (1 John 5:20). Now, circle the words "so that."

To emphasize the point John was making, what has He given us?

11. Let's take a look at one woman whose knowledge of God radically affected her future and future generations in her family tree. Read Joshua 2 and answer the following question.

The Israelites were finally ready to enter the Promised Land. Where did the spies go once they entered Jericho?

The idea of the spies going to a prostitute's house might be a little disconcerting. Here's what the *NIV Commentary* has to say: "The house of the prostitute Rahab was the only place where the men could stay with any hope of remaining undetected and where they would be able to gather the information they were seeking. Moreover, her house afforded an easy way of escape since it was located on the wall (v. 15)."[3] In those days, it was not uncommon for traveling men to stay in the house of a prostitute. The people of Jericho would not be suspicious of the men staying there. (I'm just glad we have hotels these days.)

What did Rahab say to the spies about God? (verses 8-13)

How did her knowledge of God spare her life and the life of her family? (Joshua 2:14; 6:22-23)

Because of Rahab's faith in and knowledge of God, she was grafted into the Hebrew nation. Who were some of her more famous descendants? (Matthew 1:5-16)

Rahab had been a prostitute in a heathen nation, but because of her knowledge of God and her faith in God, He showcased her as one of His mighty warriors in the Hall of Faith. Peruse the Hall of Faith in Hebrews 11 and find her name engraved on its walls.

12. Rahab had a good understanding of who God is. If someone were to ask you the question "Who is God?" what would you say?

13. How does knowing God affect your life? What difference has it made?

14. What did Jesus teach about the importance and benefits of knowing God and His Word?

    John 8:32

    John 17:3

    John 17:17 (define "sanctify")

15. How does knowing God's Word affect the way we think?

    Romans 12:2

    Philippians 1:9-10 (take note of the words "so that")

    Colossians 3:2-10 (focus on verse 10)

16. How does knowing God's Word affect the way we live?

    Psalm 119:11

    Titus 1:1

    2 Peter 1:3

17. When we become students of God's Word, we are not left alone to try to understand the Scriptures the best we can. Who comes alongside us to help us understand what God is teaching us through His Word? (John 16:13)

18. We can read a menu and even look at and smell a buffet, but until we actually put the food in our mouths and digest it, we will

still go hungry. We won't know if the food is good until we taste it. What did David challenge us to do? Read and record Psalm 34:8. Then rewrite that verse in your own words.

19. What was the frustration of the writer of Hebrews in regard to this particular church's depth of knowledge about God? (Hebrews 5:11-14)

Have you settled for milk or are you willing to chew on the meat of God's Word?

Do you require someone to spoon-feed you God's Word, or are you willing to dig into the Scriptures on your own? Friend, the mere fact that you are doing this study with me proves that you are willing to do some digging on your own! Welcome to the meat department!

20. It is not enough to merely learn God's Word. It must move from our heads to our hearts to our feet. We must apply it and walk it out in our daily lives. What is the result of practicing what we learn? (Philippians 4:9)

21. What warning does James give us against listening to the Word and not applying it to our lives? What is the result of applying what we learn in the Word to our lives? (James 1:22-25)

22. Jesus came to set women free. But with that freedom comes great responsibility. We must study the Word of God and learn how to handle it accurately. What did Paul encourage Timothy to do? (2 Timothy 2:15)

23. In *What God Really Thinks About Women*, we took an in-depth look at how God welcomed Mary of Bethany into the classroom, recorded in Luke 10:38-42. As a review, how was Mary of Bethany willing to go against the cultural norms of an all-male classroom?

24. What did Jesus say about Mary's choice to sit at the Teacher's feet to learn?

25. What did John write was his greatest joy? (3 John 1:4)

I think God would say the same about His daughters.

26. Sum up what it means to you that Jesus swung open the doors and invited women to join the classroom.

What does God really think about women? In a culture where women were not allowed to study under the rabbis' teaching, Jesus welcomed them into the classroom. He taught where women could hear: along the shore, in the marketplace, on the hillsides. In a culture that said women were unteachable, God moved them to the head of the class and made them some of His star pupils.

Lesson 9

❦

Affirmed in God's Family

hope that you have read chapters 8 and 9 in *What God Really Thinks About Women.* In our last lesson, we focused on how Jesus welcomed women into His classroom. We left Martha in the kitchen, but is that where she stayed? What does God consider a woman's most important role? Where does a woman find her significance? We'll answer all those questions and more, but let's start out with seeing how knowing Jesus changed Martha's life.

1. In order to review what we learned about Martha, read Luke 10:38-42. Looking at various Bible translations, Martha is described as bothered, worried, encumbered, captive, busy, and the jittery-type. What caused her to feel so burdened?

2. Did you notice that Martha tried to place her burden on Mary's shoulders? Have you ever felt worried and bothered about a situation and then tried to alleviate your burden by placing it on someone else? (I know that is an uncomfortable question, but please be honest.) What does that look like in your life?

3. Perhaps you have felt the weight of someone else's yoke placed on *you*. What does that feel like? (Let me tell you a little secret: False guilt sometimes holds that yoke in place.)

4. Martha had a yoke around her neck and tried to get Mary to slip into the position of the second oxen.

   What is a yoke? Look it up in the dictionary and draw a picture of a yoke fit for two oxen.

5. What happens when we yoke ourselves to Jesus, rather than to others' expectations of what we should be doing? (Matthew 11:28-30)

6. The NIV states that Martha was "distracted." The word can also mean "pulled apart" or "pulled away." What pulls you away from making spending time with Jesus your highest priority?

7. Martha no doubt felt cultural pressure to perform in a certain way. Let's ask ourselves some personal questions to help evaluate our priorities.

   Who created Martha's to-do list?

Who determines your to-do list?

Who determined Jesus' to-do list? (Mark 1:35-38; John 14:31)

How much of what Martha was doing was necessary?

How much of what you do is necessary?

8. As women, we can make ourselves very busy doing good things. However, when we let God set our priorities, we are set free to do great things. How did Paul say we could determine what is "best" for our lives? (Philippians 1:9-11)

9. What can we learn about what happened to Martha after her encounter with Jesus? Did she accept His invitation and join the classroom? Let's look at her conversation with Jesus after her brother, Lazarus, died to find out.

Read John 11:25-26 and answer the following questions.

What did Jesus teach Martha?

This is one of the most fundamental truths of the Christian faith and is often repeated at funerals to give hope to those left behind...and it was given to a woman.

What did Jesus ask Martha?

The culture believed that women could listen, but only men could learn. How did Jesus asking Martha this question go against the culture norms and show that women *must* learn?

What was her response?

How was her response similar to Peter's response recorded in Matthew 16:16?

In Jesus' response to Peter, He said, "Blessed are you, Simon son of Jonah, for this was not revealed to you by man, but by my Father in heaven. And I tell you that you are Peter [Greek, *petros* meaning "little rock or detached stone"][1] and on this rock [Greek *petra* meaning "big rock"][2] I will build my church and the gates of Hades will not overcome it" (Matthew 16:17-18).

How exciting that one of the foundational truths of our faith was voiced by both a man and a woman. How precious that God made sure both statements were included in the Bible. Why is that significant against this particular cultural backdrop?

10. Did Martha become comfortable with Mary being Mary and letting Martha be Martha? How does John 12:2 give you a hint?

11. During Jesus' day a woman's significance was wrapped up in being a wife and a mother. (In many cases, that attitude is not much different today.) But Jesus taught that a woman's significance wasn't dependent on either role. Her significance was wrapped up in who she was as a child of God (Luke 11:27-28).

Jesus did not speak about being single specifically, but there were several significant people in His life who were never married. As far as we know, neither Mary nor Martha were married. Jesus Himself was single.

Paul spoke specifically to single women. What did he tell them? (1 Corinthians 7:32-35)

(Don't get hung up on Paul's idea that it is good to stay single. In 1 Timothy 4:1-3 he wrote that in the latter days, "some will abandon the faith and follow deceiving spirits and things taught by demons. Such teachings come through hypocritical liars, whose consciences have been seared as with a hot iron. They forbid people to marry." Paul didn't teach not to marry; rather, he simply saw that an unmarried person would be better able to concentrate all his/her energies on building the kingdom. But I love marriage! So does God. It was His idea.)

12. Now let's look at how several single women impacted God's kingdom. Here are some ladies I'd like you to meet.

Corrie ten Boom was held captive in a German death camp for many years. From the time of her release in 1944 until her death in 1983, she traveled the world, speaking in 60 countries and telling others about how God forgives our sins and throws them into the deepest of seas...even the sins of a Nazi soldier who approached her after speaking to a crowd. Her book and subsequent movie, *The Hiding Place,* were both released after her eightieth birthday. In the first five months, more than 9 million people watched the film. She never married. She had great significance in the kingdom of God.

Lottie Moon gave her life as a missionary in China as a teacher and evangelist. At age 14, Lottie went to school at Virginia Female Seminary and later at Albemarle Female Institute in Charlottesville, Virginia. In 1861 Lottie received one of the first master of arts degrees awarded to a woman by a Southern institution. She spoke numerous languages: Latin, Greek, French, Italian, Spanish, and Chinese. During a time when it was unheard of for a woman to be a missionary in a foreign country, Lottie set her sights on China. At age 33 she moved to China to "go out among the millions" as an evangelist, only to find herself relegated to teaching a school of 40 "unstudious" children. She felt chained down and came to view herself as part of an oppressed class—single women missionaries. Her writings were an appeal on behalf of all those who were facing similar situations in their ministries. Lottie waged a slow but relentless campaign to give women missionaries the freedom to minister and have an equal voice in mission proceedings. A prolific writer, she corresponded frequently with H.A. Tupper, head of the Southern Baptist Foreign Mission Board, informing him of the realities of mission work and the desperate need for more workers—both women and men. Lottie Moon gave her life to evangelize the Chinese people, and the Southern Baptists, even today, collect "The Lottie Moon offering" at Christmastime to help support foreign missions. Lottie Moon never married. She had great significance in the kingdom of God.

Henrietta Mears was a well-known teacher at Hollywood

Presbyterian church in Hollywood, California. She mentored Billy Graham, Dr. Bill Bright (founder of Campus Crusade for Christ), and a former chaplain of the U.S. Senate, Dr. Richard Halverson. Henrietta, often referred to as simply "Teacher," was the person chiefly responsible for leading Bill Bright to Christ during her teaching Bible study groups in her home. She was also the founder of Gospel Light Press, a leading publisher of Christian education material. On my shelf I have one of her classics, *What the Bible Is All About.* Henrietta Mears never married. She had great significance in the kingdom of God.

I could give many more examples of the great significance single women have had and continue to have in building God's kingdom. These are just three. And if you are single and holding this book in your hands, you are another one.

13. Now let's turn our attention to another area in which women tried (and still try) to find significance—motherhood. In Jesus' time a woman's worth was determined by whether or not she could bear children—more specifically, male children to continue the family name. What do the following Old Testament verses tell us about women who struggled with infertility?

Genesis 11:30

Genesis 30:1

1 Samuel 1:2,10-11

14. When Elizabeth finally conceived, what did she call her decades of barrenness? (Luke 1:25)

    It was a common belief in those days that infertility was a punishment. However, how was Elizabeth described? (Luke 1:6)

15. Let's see what Jesus had to say about where a woman's significance came from. Read Luke 11:27-28. What did the woman in the crowd cry out?

    What was Jesus' response?

    What can you surmise is a woman's most fulfilling role in life?

In Jesus' response, He catapulted women to the position of disciple, along with the men who had followed Him all along. He made it clear that a woman's significance rested in being a child of God.

16. One day, after Jesus had sent out the disciples, they were ecstatic that the spirits obeyed them. However, Jesus reminded them that their significance didn't lie in what they did. What did He tell them was the ultimate reason for rejoicing? (Luke 10:17-20)

How does that same source of significance apply to you?

17. When God created Adam and Eve, He commanded them, "Be fruitful and multiply, and fill the earth, and subdue it" (Genesis 1:28 NASB). In the New Testament, Jesus also talked about being fruitful and multiplying, but in a different sense. What did Jesus tell His disciples to do? (Matthew 28:18-20)

    Jesus commissions all of us to share the gospel. Once someone accepts Christ as Savior and becomes a Christ-follower, what is that person then called?

    2 Corinthians 6:18

    Ephesians 5:1

    1 John 3:1

    How can each of us be fruitful and multiply in the kingdom of God?

18. As a woman of great significance to God, take a look at how you are described in Paul's letters and the teachings of Jesus. Look up

the following verses and note who you are—your true identity in Christ. Write what you think each particular role entails.

Matthew 5:13

Matthew 5:14

John 15:16

Romans 8:17

1 Corinthians 3:16

2 Corinthians 2:15

2 Corinthians 5:20

Ephesians 1:11

Ephesians 2:10

2 Timothy 2:3

Hebrews 12:1

19. Colossians 2:10 says the following: "In Him you have been made complete" (NASB). What does it mean to you to be complete in Christ?

20. Ponder these words by Carolyn Custis James: "A woman's high calling as God's image bearer renders her incapable of insignificance, no matter what has gone wrong in her life or how much she has lost."[3] What does that mean to you?

21. In no way is this lesson intended to diminish the importance of being a wife and a mother. Those have been two of the most important roles of my life. Being an *ezer* to my husband is an honor I do not take lightly. Being a mother to my son has been one of my greatest joys. To think that God gives a mother the privilege of shaping and molding a child, an eternal soul, for a very short, very fleeting period of time is simply mind-boggling. But if our significance is wrapped up in any person other than God and in who we are as His child, we will be disappointed and dissatisfied.

Write a summary statement about what determines your true significance as a woman.

What does God really think about women? Women have great significance to God because they are His female image bearers. Your significance is bound up in the fact that you are deeply loved, completely forgiven, fully pleasing, and totally accepted by God through Jesus Christ. As a Christian, you are equipped by God, empowered by the Holy Spirit, and enveloped in Jesus Christ. Now that's something to get excited about.

Lesson 10

CALLED OUT OF THE SHADOWS

In lesson 6 we took a bird's-eye view of women Jesus restored in His ministry. Today, let's zoom in on one particular woman to see how God called her out of the shadows and onto center stage. In chapter 10 of *What God Really Thinks About Women*, we spend some time with the woman with the crippled back. Today, let's go back to the synagogue and take a closer look at the verbs or action words used in that passage. Read Luke 13:10-17 to refresh your memory. Concentrate on the actions of Jesus.

Jesus Saw Her

1. First of all, Jesus saw her. She did not see Him, but He saw her. Read the following verses and note what you learn about what or who God sees.

   Psalm 33:13-15,18

   Psalm 121:3-4,7-8

   Matthew 6:3-4,6

2. Hagar was a young woman in a terrible situation. She was pregnant and mistreated by the only family she had. Read Genesis 16 and answer the following questions.

   Where did Hagar run?

   After the angel's pronouncement, what name did Hagar call God and why?

   "El Roi" means "the God Who Sees." What does that particular name for God mean to you?

   How does the fact that God sees you make you feel?

3. What did David say about what God sees? (Psalm 139)

4. No matter what you are going through today, know this: God sees you. He has not forgotten you. What reassurance does He give us in the words of Isaiah 49:15-16?

Jesus Called Her Forward

5. The Greek word for "called," *kaleo,* means "to call or invite." But it also means a spiritual calling to salvation, serving God and

fellow believers. Read the following verses and note what you learn about your calling as a believer.

Romans 1:6

1 Corinthians 1:9

1 Thessalonians 2:11-12

1 Thessalonians 4:7

2 Timothy 1:8-10

1 Peter 2:9

2 Peter 1:3

6. Fulfilling a calling (or accepting God's invitation) usually involves getting out of our comfort zones. In my own life, I can't think of a time when obeying Him didn't. How did the woman with the crippled back have to move out of her comfort zone? (Luke 13:12)

7. How did each one of the following women have to move out of their comfort zones to follow God?

Sarah, the wife of Abraham (Genesis 12:1)

Ruth (Ruth 2:1-3)

Esther (Esther 4, focusing on verses 12-16)

Mary Magdalene (Luke 8:1-3)

The woman with the 12-year bleeding (Luke 8:40-48)

Mary of Bethany (Luke 10:38-39)

The Samaritan woman at the well (John 4:28-30)

Are you operating in your comfort zone, or have you ventured out to areas where you are totally dependent on God's power and might?

8. Why do you think God moves us out of our comfort zones to accomplish great feats for Him?

9. We've looked at this verse in a previous lesson, but refresh your memory and read and record what Paul says about weakness versus strength in 2 Corinthians 12:9-10.

10. Read 1 Corinthians 1:26-31. What does God use to shame the wise?

What does God use to shame the strong?

I don't know about you, but 1 Corinthians 1:26-31 describes me to a T.

Here's how Eugene Peterson paraphrases those verses in modern day language:

> Take a good look, friends, at who you were when you got called into this life. I don't see many of "the brightest and the best" among you, not many influential, not many from high-society families. Isn't it obvious that God deliberately chose men and women that the culture overlooks and exploits and abuses, chose these "nobodies" to expose the hollow pretensions of the "somebodies"? That makes it quite clear that none of you can get by with blowing your own horn before God. Everything that we have—right thinking and right living, a clean slate and a fresh start—comes

from God by way of Jesus Christ. That's why we have the saying, "If you're going to blow a horn, blow a trumpet for God" (MSG).

Amen to that!

I am sure the crippled woman felt very insignificant. I'm sure she felt like a "nobody." And in the eyes of the world, that's exactly what she was. But to Jesus, she was a precious jewel.

11. Read Hebrews 11:8 and note how Abraham responded to God's call. Do you think this woman knew why Jesus was calling her forward? And yet what did she do?

12. What is the assurance for all of us who are called? (Romans 8:28)

Jesus Spoke to Her

13. Does Jesus still speak to us today? (John 10:14,27)

14. What did God tell us to do in regard to Jesus' words? (Mark 9:7)

15. One of the most important ways that God speaks today is through His Word. Give an example of how God has spoken to you specifically through the Bible. Consider Psalm 119:105.

16. Author Ken Gire asks, "Should we even expect Him to speak in the everyday moments of our lives? Or should we be content with echoes, however eloquent, from the past? If God does still speak, perhaps some of those words are words for us. Perhaps He is offering us in themed afternoons of our lives small slices of heaven to stave off the hunger—or maybe arouse it."[1]

Have you been content listening to what others have heard, or are you hungry to hear from God directly?

Jesus Touched Her

17. I love the thought of Jesus' hands reaching out and touching the people He came in contact with. The leprous outcast, the unclean recluse, the deceased son, the dead little girl...each person Jesus touched was changed by the hands of heaven...the fingertips of God.

Look up the following verses and note the people Jesus touched and what happened to them.

Matthew 8:2-3

Matthew 8:14-15

Matthew 9:27-30

Mark 7:31-35

Luke 7:11-15

Luke 8:51-55

18. Jesus healed people with His words. "Be clean!" He spoke to the man who suffered from leprosy (Matthew 8:3). He healed him physically with His words, but I believe Jesus healed the hurt in his soul with His touch. Can you think of a time when someone's touch ministered to you? A hug? A pat on the back? A touch of the hand?

Jesus touched the untouchables of the world. Will you do the same?

Jesus Affirmed Her

19. What did Jesus call the woman with the crippled back? (Luke 13:16)

As we learned in lesson 4, it was common for Jewish men to be called "sons of Abraham." This would imply that the Jewish male inherited the promises as a son of the Old Testament covenant. However, it was unheard of for a Jewish woman to be referred to as a "daughter of Abraham."

How would those words have affirmed her significance?

20. Read Romans 8:16 and note what God calls you.

21. How would it have affirmed her to know that Jesus stopped right in the middle of His teaching to take notice of her?

Jesus Healed Her

22. There is much we could say about Jesus healing people, but there is one specific aspect I want us to look at together. Read Matthew 14:14. How did Jesus feel when He saw the crowds that had followed Him?

23. The Bible says, "He had compassion on them." The Greek word used for "compassion" in this passage is *splanchnizomai.* If you happen to be in the medical profession, that word might look familiar. Splanchnology is the study of the visceral parts—in common terms, the gut. The verb "carries the idea of being moved in the inner parts of the body. The ancients thought of the inward parts of the body as being the seat of emotions. In English, we usually refer to the 'heart,' but we also talk of a person having 'visceral' feelings; note how true compassion can affect us in the pit of our stomachs."[2]

Look up the following verses and note what moved Jesus in the very pit of His stomach.

Matthew 9:36

Matthew 15:32

Matthew 20:34

Mark 1:41

Mark 6:34

Mark 8:2

Luke 7:13

24. Jesus felt the limp of the crippled woman. He felt the rejection of the woman at the well. He felt the loneliness of the woman labeled unclean because of bleeding. Does this give you a better idea of how Jesus' heart ached because of the sickness, disease, heartache, and hunger He saw?

What does Hebrews 13:8 tell you about Him?

If Jesus felt *splanchnizomai,* gut-wrenching compassion, for the people He saw when he walked the earth, how does He feel about the pain you suffer today? (Hebrews 13:8)

25. Record the six action words we discovered in Jesus' interaction with the woman with the crippled back. How has Jesus acted in those same six ways in your own life?

26. Dear friend, now I want you to picture yourself sitting behind the partition at the back of the temple with the woman with the crippled back. Jesus stops midsentence, sees *you,* calls to *you,* speaks to *you,* touches *your* soul to take away *your* pain, affirms *you* as a child of God, and then heals *you.* What feelings stir in your heart as you walk in her footsteps?

*What does God really think about women? He loves them
so much that He sent His Son to let them know that He sees
them, calls to them, speaks to them, touches them, affirms
them, and heals them as His daughters. Jesus stopped
right in the middle of His teaching to take care of one lone
woman. He loved her that much. He loves you that much.*

HIGHLIGHTED IN THE OLD TESTAMENT

don't know about you, but like the Syrophoenician mother, I have fallen at Jesus' feet many times in prayer for the needs of my family. As a woman, it's what we do—bring our loved ones before God and pray for His intervention. As our Savior, it's what Jesus does—listens to our hearts and intercedes on our behalf. In *What God Really Thinks About Women*, we have enjoyed getting to know many of the leading ladies of the New Testament. In this lesson, let's turn back time even further and meet a few of the leading ladies of the Old Testament.

1. Read Ruth 1:1-5. From these five verses, list the six people you meet.

   Now draw a line through those who had died by the end of verse 5. Whom do you have left?

2. From the very beginning of the book of Ruth, we see that this is a story about women. While most of the other women in the Old Testament enter their particular stories on the arm of a man, we see these three women taking center stage alone. Continue reading verses 6-13.

   What was Naomi's desire for her daughters-in-law?

   Why did she want them to return to their homeland rather than continue on to Bethlehem with her?

3. What did the two daughters-in-law decide to do? (verses 14-18)

   What does this tell you about the source of Ruth's identity and significance?

   What was important to her?

4. What did both Ruth and Naomi have in common?

5. Not only was Ruth a young widow, she was also apparently barren. What did this mean for her future?

Who would take care of her?

Did she seem concerned?

Why or why not?

6. How did Naomi view her present state? (verses 20-21)

7. Naomi felt as though God had forsaken her, but in reality He was working behind the scenes to put every detail in place. Why? Because God loves His daughters that much. When Ruth went to glean in the fields the following day, where did she "just so happen" to go? (Ruth 2:1-9,19-20)

   How did this revelation change Naomi's opinion about God? (verse 20)

8. Have you ever gone through a difficult time and felt God had deserted you? Then, after the situation was resolved, you discovered God's fingerprints all over the details? If so, give an example.

9. Read through Ruth 3. Compare what Naomi told Ruth to say to Boaz, with what Ruth actually said to Boaz. Specifically note verses 3-4 and verse 9.

   What does this tell you about Ruth's gumption?

10. What heroic qualities have you seen in Ruth thus far? Make a list.

    Was she a woman of strength or weakness?

    Did she take initiative or wait for others to act?

    Was she timid or a woman of great courage?

    Was she overly cautious or a risk-taker?

    How did she demonstrate the qualities of an *ezer* that we saw in chapter 1 of *What God Really Thinks About Women*?

11. What was the final result of the strength and courage exhibited in these two heroines in the book of Ruth? (Ruth 4:13-22)

We would be missing a vital point if we saw the book of Ruth as a simple love story. In reality, this is a story of two women—two heroines—that God used to preserve the royal line of David from which our Savior would be born. Amazing.

12. Describe any area of your life where you need to be more like Ruth—bolder for God.

13. In the Old Testament, God often invited women to participate in His exploits. While the culture may have sequestered women behind the curtain as stagehands, God placed them in starring roles. Ruth and Naomi are two examples. Now let's turn back even further, to the days of the great Exodus. Read Exodus 1–2:10 and note how God used each of the women mentioned. Explain how each one of these women showed great courage.

The Hebrew midwives

Jacobed (Moses' mother)

Miriam (Moses' sister)

Pharaoh's daughter

14. Later, God recounted His bringing the Israelites out of Egypt through the prophet Micah. Who did God name as the leaders of the Exodus? (Micah 6:4)

15. Moses married a woman named Zipporah. To give you a little background, God had given Moses the command to circumcise all Hebrew males as a sign of the covenant between God and His chosen people. However, Moses failed to circumcise his own son. How did Moses' wife take initiative to save her husband from God's wrath? This is not a very pretty picture, but it shows how God used a woman to intervene for her husband. (Exodus 4:24-26)

16. Read Judges 4:4-10. Who was leading Israel at the time?

What were some of her duties? (Judges 4:4-6,9; 5:1)

Note how one of her duties was similar to Moses'. (Exodus 18:13,15)

Deborah means "bee" and she was certainly a busy bee. (Just a note on Deborah's warning to Barak that a woman would get all the glory if she went with him into battle. She was not referring to herself, but to Jael mentioned in Judges 4:21. Not exactly children's bedtime story material.)

17. Let's look at another courageous Old Testament heroine. Read 1 Samuel 25 and answer the following questions.

    Who was Abigail? How was she described? (verse 3)

    How was her husband described? (verses 2-3)

    What was David going to do after his rejection by Nabal? (verses 7-13)

    How did Abigail use wisdom in her humble approach to David? (verses 18-31)

    What did David say about her character? (verse 33)

    How did the Lord deal with Abigail's foolish husband? (verses 36-38)

    What can we learn from Abigail's courage?

18. Let's look at one more Old Testament heroine in our journey to discover what God really thinks about women. Esther was a little orphaned Jewish girl who was called out of the shadows and

placed in the spotlight of God's redemptive plan. Because of her inner and outer beauty, she was chosen to be queen of a heathen nation. But with that honor, a terrifying opportunity arose. The entire Hebrew nation was facing annihilation because of one jealous man named Haman. He issued a king-approved edict that, on a particular day, all the Jews were going to be killed. Esther, whom no one in the royal court knew was a Jew, was in a position to possibly stop it. However, if she went before the king to plead for her people, and the king was not pleased with her, he could have her killed. Read her cousin Mordecai's response to her fears. (Esther 4:12-14)

How did this courageous woman respond? (Esther 4:15-16; scan Esther 5, 7, and 8:1-10)

What was the outcome of her courageous move to come out of the shadows and speak to the king? (Esther 9)

How does this story confirm Acts 17:26?

These leading ladies of the Old Testament showed great courage as they trusted God. One thing that jumped out at me during my study of them is that while women leaders were not common, when they did appear, there is not an ounce of shock at their appearance. There is no indication that they were an exception or an abnormality. The writers note the accounts of their exploits as though they were not unusual or looked down upon.

*What does God really think about women? We can
discover what God thinks about women through the
life of Jesus, His Son. We can also catch glimpses of how
God cherishes His female image bearers in how He
gave them leading roles in the Old Testament as well.*

Empowered by the Holy Spirit

One thing I just love about the story of the widow who gave her two mites is the fact that she gave all she had. She didn't have much to give, but then again, Jesus doesn't need much to work with. He fed 5000 men plus women and children with two loaves of bread and five fish, He served up robust wine with two large jars of water, and He changed the world with just a handful of uneducated fishermen. All He needs is a heart that is committed to Him.

Like the widow with the two mites, you might not feel that you have much to offer, but God would not agree. You have been equipped by Him and empowered by the Holy Spirit! Let's spend this lesson taking a look at how God has equipped and empowered women to impact the world for Christ.

1. Before Jesus left the disciples to make His way to the cross, He promised them that He would not leave them alone. Read the following verses and note what Jesus taught about the Holy Spirit.

   Luke 11:11-13

John 14:15-26

John 16:7-15

2. Who was present in the room where the disciples waited for the Holy Spirit? (Acts 1:12-14)

3. Who was present and filled when the Holy Spirit descended at Pentecost? (Acts 2:1-4; 2:14-18)

4. When Peter stood to explain what was happening, he announced that what they were seeing was a fulfillment of Joel's prophecy in Joel 2:28-32. Who was included in this prophecy and in its fulfillment on the day of Pentecost?

5. One function of the Holy Spirit is that He gives spiritual gifts to believers. Read the following passages and make a list of the gifts of the Spirit. As you are reading these verses, also look for the purposes for the spiritual gifts.

Romans 12:3-8

1 Corinthians 12:4-11

1 Corinthians 12:27-31

Ephesians 4:11-16

The gifts overlap in various lists. Some theologians break them down into ministry gifts and motivational gifts. Some people may have more than one. But Scripture is clear that every Christian has a spiritual gift (1 Corinthians 12:11). Remember, the gifts of the Spirit are called "gifts," which means we don't earn them. They are given to us as a gift. How useful is a gift if you never unwrap it and take it out of the box?

6. Did you notice any gender specifications for the gifts? That is, did Paul say that some gifts were for women and some were for men?

7. What two spiritual gifts were women practicing in the Corinthian church as noted in 1 Corinthians 11:5?

8. What three purposes for prophecy did Paul mention in 1 Corinthians 14:3?

9. The church in Corinth was a disorderly mess. What three areas of confusion did Paul address in 1 Corinthians 14:26-35?

What did he say about the women?

But wait! Didn't Paul already mention that women were prophesying and praying in church? Let's dig deeper. If we ever sense that the Bible is contradicting itself, it means that we don't have a complete understanding of what God is really saying.

We must remember that much of what is written in the letters to the churches were to address specific problems. In this case, there was disorder and confusion. Women were talking in church, chatting with each other and asking their husbands questions about what was going on. The women were uneducated in the Scriptures and proper worship decorum, whereas the men had been taught these things all their lives. If Paul meant women should be totally silent, then it would mean no singing, repeating a creed, praying, making an announcement, or giving a testimony. The verse could better be translated "stop talking in church."

The Message says it this way: "Wives must not disrupt worship, talking when they should be listening, asking questions that could more appropriately be asked of their husbands at home. God's Book of the law guides our manners and customs here. Wives have no license to use the time of worship for unwarranted speaking" (1 Corinthians 14:34-35).

In *Christianity Today*, theologian Kenneth S. Kantzer wrote, "In 1 Corinthians 12, we are caught in an intricate interplay between quotations from a missing letter from the Corinthians and Paul's solutions to the problems the letter had raised. The verse is clearly not repeating a law of Scripture and cannot be taken as a universal command for women to be 'silent in the church.' That interpretation would flatly contradict what the apostle had just said three chapters earlier."[1]

I think of it this way. In Paul's letters, when he is addressing a problem in a particular church, it is as though we are listening to one side of a phone conversation. In light of 1 Corinthians 11:5, 1 Corinthians 14:34 could not mean total silence.

10. What was Paul's summary statement in 1 Corinthians 14:40? What was his main concern?

Even though Paul corrected these three areas of disorder in the Corinthian church, he did not take away the worshippers' newfound freedom, nor did he permanently silence them.

11. Just as a reminder, what did the prophet Joel say would be happening in the last days? (Joel 2:28-29)

12. What does 1 Peter 4:10-11 tell us about the purposes of the gifts of the Spirit?

13. Read the parable found in Matthew 25:14-30 and answer the following questions.

With whom was the master pleased?

With whom was the master not pleased?

In one word, why did the servant with only one talent hide it?

In regard to your own spiritual "talents" and gifts, what can you glean from this parable?

14. One of Paul's terms for those who worked with him in ministry was "coworker." The Greek word for "coworker" is *synergos*. This word looks much like the English word "synergy." Look up the definition of "synergy" in an English dictionary. What do you learn about the combined effort of two or more people working together?

15. In some churches in China, they welcome new believers by saying "Jesus now has a new pair of eyes to see with, new ears to listen with, new hands to help with, and a new heart to love others with."[2] How does 1 Corinthians 12:12-27 support that statement?

To help you remember this important concept, record 1 Corinthians 12:27.

16. If there is one thing I have learned, it is that God does not always call the qualified, but He always qualifies the called. Consider this: Rahab was a harlot, Miriam was a gossip, Sarah was a doubter, and Bathsheba (who most likely wrote Proverbs 31:10-31) was an adulteress. Mary Magdalene was a demoniac, Martha was a worrywart, the woman with the bleeding was a recluse, the woman at the well was a five-time divorcee, the Syrophoenician

mom was insecure, the woman who anointed Jesus with oil had a sinful past, and the widow with the two coins was poor.

So, what's holding you back?

17. If you have left your spiritual gift or gifts on a shelf and they have become a bit dusty, consider taking them down and dusting them off. What did Paul tell his friend Timothy to do with his spiritual gift that had perhaps grown a bit cold? (2 Timothy 1:6)

If you are doing this study in a group study, consider partnering with another woman and fanning your spiritual gifts into a blaze! Ask each other:

What is your spiritual gift or gifts?

How are you using your spiritual gift or gifts?

If you are not using your spiritual gift or gifts as this time, what are you going to do to change that?

18. In summary, how has God equipped women to impact the world for Christ?

19. Here's one more verse I want you to ponder. Acts 4:13 tells the key to the uneducated disciples' success and the key to our success as well. Read the verse and fill in the blanks. "And they took note _____ _____ _____ _____ _____ _____ _____."

What does God really think about women? He empowers and equips Christian women with spiritual gifts to share the hope and healing of Christ with a hurting world and to build His kingdom on earth. He calls them to operate in the body of Christ—to be His hands, feet, legs, arms, eyes, ears, and mouthpiece.

CHOSEN FOR
SUCH A TIME AS THIS

can hardly believe we are at the end of our journey together. In our final moments, I long for you to know that God has an incredible plan for you. Just like any good father, He has dreams for His precious daughters—that includes *you*. Jesus said, "I have come that they might have life, and have it to the full" (John 10:10). For a woman, or for any follower of Christ, that is not a life of rule-following dos and don'ts, repetitive religious rhetoric, or long-faced piety. It is a "wonderful adventure to be viewed each day on tiptoe, radiantly discovering God's Word and His ways. It is choosing to see a sovereign hand guiding, coaxing, pausing, and blessing you to the fulfillment of His purposes in your life."[1]

So let's turn our attention now to some of Jesus' final words and how we, as God's girls, can help fulfill the Great Commission in our lifetime.

1. When studying the Gospels, I was struck with how many times Jesus told His followers to "go." I have a beautiful picture in my mind of Jesus placing His hands on the shoulders of our healed and forgiven heroines, turning them around to face their futures, and pointing them forward to change the world.

Look up the following verses and note when Jesus said "Go." What did He tell each person to go and do? We're going to look at some of our brothers too.

Matthew 28:16-20

Mark 5:18-20

Mark 5:34

Luke 7:50

Luke 8:47-48

John 8:11

From these passages, what can we summarize about what Jesus calls us to do once He has transformed our lives?

2. When Jesus healed the woman with the issue of blood, what did He push her to do? (Luke 8:45-48)

When Jesus confronted the Samaritan woman at the well, what was she compelled to do? (John 4:28-29).

When Jesus appeared to Mary Magdalene, what did He commission her to do? (John 20:17)

3. Read and record Revelation 12:10-11. Who is the "him" in verse 11?

Why would the enemy want you to keep quiet about what God has done in your life?

4. What did Jesus tell the disciples in John 4:34-38?

Statistics show that approximately two-thirds of Christians today are women. That means there are a lot of female workers who could be bringing in the harvest. How will you respond to Jesus' call to "go and tell"?

5. What happened after Jesus' resurrection? Did the disciples continue with Jesus' example of valuing and respecting women as co-image bearers of God? Did they continue allowing women

to walk through the doors Jesus had swung wide open? One of the best-kept secrets is the impact women had in the growth and establishment of the early church. Let's spend some time discovering the part women played.

At Pentecost, recorded in Acts 2, Peter preached his first sermon empowered by the Holy Spirit. How many were added to the church that day? (Acts 2:40-41)

How does the numbering of those added to the church in Acts 2:40-41 differ from the numbering of those who were fed during Jesus' miraculous feeding of the multitudes in Matthew 14:13-21 (note verse 21)? Matthew 15:32-38 (note verse 38)? Mark 6:30-44 (note verse 44)? Mark 8:1-9 (note verse 9). Who *was not* included in the numbering of the miraculous feedings of the Gospels and *who* was included in the miraculous conversion in Acts?

6. Read Acts 9:32-42 and answer the following questions.

   How did Luke, the author of the book of Acts, describe Tabitha (sometimes called Dorcas)?

   What happened to her?

   Who traveled and asked for Peter to come?

What occurred as a result of Peter's visit?

Given the circumstances surrounding this event, would you say that Dorcas was a significant or insignificant person in the establishment and growth of the church in Joppa?

7. When we are first introduced to Paul in the book of Acts, his name is Saul and he is known for persecuting and arresting Christians. Who did Saul have arrested in Acts 9:2?

What does the fact that Saul had women arrested tell you about the impact he felt they were having on the growth and spread of the gospel?

8. After Saul's miraculous conversion on the road to Damascus, God changed his name to Paul (Acts 9). On his second missionary journey, he traveled to Philippi. With whom did Paul share the gospel when he first arrived? (Acts 16:13-15)

Lydia, a woman, was the first convert on Paul's journey to Europe. Let's keep walking with Paul. Who was the second person Paul ministered to in Philippi? (Acts 16:16-18)

Who was the third person to be added to the church at Philippi? (Acts 16:29-34)

Now, describe the church of Philippi so far.

9. Many have suggested that Paul continued the tradition of suppressing and oppressing women. Some have even called him a "woman hater." But nothing could be further from the truth. He understood the great impact women had on the growth of the Christian faith even before he gave his life to Christ. After his conversion, Paul continued in the example of Jesus by including women in key leadership roles in the church.

He recognized women as coheirs with Christ and recipients of the Holy Spirit who would partner with men to spread the gospel and build the church throughout the world.

Whom did Paul preach to in Thessalonica and Berea? (Acts 17:4,12)

10. Read the following verses and note what you learn about two of Paul's closest ministry partners.

Acts 18:18-19,26

Romans 16:3

1 Corinthians 16:19

2 Timothy 4:19

11. How were Philip's daughters described? (Acts 21:8-9)

12. At the end of Paul's letter to the Romans, he created quite a list of men and women who had helped him further the gospel. Of the 29 he listed, 9 were women. List each woman and what you learn about her.

Romans 16:1 (The Greek word "servant" that it used of Phoebe is *diakonos* and is also translated "deacon" in 1 Timothy 3:8.)

Romans 16:3

Romans 16:6

Romans 16:7 (Most commentaries agree that Junias is a feminine name.)

Romans 16:12 (These two women were possibly twins as it was common for twins to have names from the same root.)

Romans 16:13

Romans 16:15

From this list, what can you surmise about women involved in Paul's ministry?

13. That same Greek word, *diaokonos,* was also used when speaking of Mary Magdalene and the women who traveled with Jesus. As a review, what did Luke say about these women? (Luke 8:3)

The word "helping" can also be translated "ministering." Both are the same Greek word.

14. Paul mentioned women and their involvement in the spread of the gospel and growth of the church in other places as well. Look up the following and note who they were and what they did.

Philippians 4:3

Colossians 4:15

Paul uses the words "struggled beside me" (NRSV) in describing Eudia and Synthych. The Greek word translated "struggle" is *synēthlēsan* and it means "to contend, as an athlete strained every muscle to achieve victory in the games. So with equal dedication these women contended with zeal for the victory of the gospel at Philippi. He places them right alongside other workers listed in the letter."[2]

15. As the curtain rises to reveal part 2 of Jesus' story and the formation of the Christian church, the lists of women abound. In the book of Acts, Luke is careful to place women at each stage in the narrative of the church's growth and expansion: Jerusalem (Acts 5:14); Samaria (8:12); and the cites of Philippi (16:13-15), Thessalonica (17:4), Berea (17:10-12), Athens (17:34), and Corinth (18:1-2). God's female image bearers had great impact in the establishment and growth of the early church. When God said, "It is not good for the man to be alone," that included building God's kingdom as well.

    Summarize what you have learned about the importance of women in the spread of the gospel, the growth of the church, and the support of Paul's ministry.

16. So, what does God really think about women? Let's take a few moments to review what we've learned about the leading ladies in the Gospels. Read the following and fill in the blanks.

    _____ was the first person in the New Testament to be told of God's redemptive plan through Jesus. (Luke 1:26-38)

    _____ was the first person to prophesy in the book of Luke. (Luke 1:41-45)

    _____ was the person to initiate Jesus' first miracle. (John 2:1-11)

    _____ was the first Samaritan convert. (John 4:7-42)

_____ was the first evangelist to the Samaritan people. (John 4:7-42)

_____ was the first person to hear Jesus state His true identity. (John 4:7-42)

_____ was the first to hear Jesus' explicit teaching on the resurrection of believers. (John 11:21-27)

_____ was the first person to prepare Jesus for burial. (Mark 14:1-9)

_____ was the first person to experience Jesus raising a loved one from the dead. (Luke 7:11-15)

_____ were the first to discover the empty tomb. (Matthew 28:1-7; Mark 16:1)

_____ was the first person to see the resurrected Jesus. (John 20:10-17)

_____ was the first person commissioned to tell of the resurrection. (John 20:17)

(Don't let it throw you that the four Gospels vary a little on which women were actually there on the morning they discovered the empty tomb. Each Gospel writer wrote what he felt was important. While Matthew, Mark, Luke, and John vary on the combination of women present, each wrote that Mary Magdalene was the first person to see the resurrected Jesus and the first one to tell the good news. That was a significant aspect of the story and included by all four writers.)

17. Who was a part of Jesus' traveling ministry team? (Luke 8:1-3)

18. With whom did Jesus have His longest recorded conversation? (John 4:1-26)

19. Who followed Jesus as He carried the cross to Calvary? (Luke 23:27)

20. Who was at the cross when Jesus died? (Mark 15:40-41)

21. Who followed Nicodemus and the Roman soldier to the tomb where Jesus was laid? (Mark 15:47)

22. What was the first word Jesus spoke after His resurrection? (John 20:15)

23. Who was present with the disciples as they waited for the gift of the Holy Spirit? (Acts 1:14)

I hope you are feeling really loved about now. Isn't it thrilling to see all these facts about the women in Jesus' ministry in one place?

24. Read Ephesians 2:10. What does Paul call you? (So the next time

someone calls you a piece of work, you can certainly agree. You are God's masterpiece.)

What does Paul tell us about one of our created purposes?

When were those specific purposes for our lives determined?

25. What do we learn in Acts 17:26 about the times and places God has ordained for us?

God has predetermined the very time and place where you live. They are no accident. You are called for such a time as this. "Long before you were conceived by your parents, you were conceived in the mind of God."[3] He has specific work for you to do. It may be to impact a child, a neighbor, a community, a nation. There are no small assignments in God's eyes. We are not called to be merely spectators to what God is doing in the world but participants. He works through His people to accomplish His purposes.

What does God really think about you? You are a woman—the inspiration for divine poetry and the grand masterpiece of God's creative genius. You are created in the image of God for a divine purpose. Make no mistake about it—God adores you. No eye has seen, no ear has heard, and no mind has conceived all that He has planned for you. You were chosen for such a time as this.

Notes

Introduction—A New Day for Women

1. Sharon Jaynes, *What God Really Thinks About Women* (Eugene, OR: Harvest House Publishers, 2010), 218.

Lesson 1—Created for Divine Purpose

1. Gilbert Bilezikian, *Beyond Sex Roles* (Grand Rapids, MI: Baker Academic, 2006), 17.
2. Kenneth Barker, General Editor, *NIV Study Bible* (Grand Rapids, MI: Zondervan Publishing House 1995), 1770.
3. Rick Warren, *The Purpose Driven® Life* (Grand Rapids, MI: Zondervan Publishing House, 2002), 55.

Lesson 2—Blessed Through Radical Obedience

1. W.E. Vine, Merrill F. Unger, William White Jr., *Vine's Complete Expository Dictionary of Old and New Testament Words* (Nashville, TN: Thomas Nelson Publishers, 1985), 73.
2. Genesis 2:5-6: "Now no shrub of the field was yet in the earth, and no plant of the field had yet sprouted, for the LORD God had not sent rain upon the earth; and there was no man to cultivate the ground. But a mist used to rise from the earth and water the whole surface of the ground" (NASB). Charles Ryrie notes in reference to Genesis 1:7: "Apparently God suspended a vast body of water in vapor form over the earth, making a canopy that caused conditions on the earth to resemble those inside a greenhouse. This may account for the longevity of human life and for the tremendous amount of water involved in the worldwide flood." In reference to Genesis 2:5-6, he notes the following about the mist: "Probably caused by daily evaporation and condensation, which occurred because of the change in temperature between daytime and nighttime." Charles Ryrie, *The Ryrie Study Bible* (Chicago, IL: Moody Publishers, 1976), 8,10.

Lesson 3—Commissioned to Go and Tell

1. Bruce Marchiano, *Jesus, the Man Who Loved Women* (New York, NY: Howard Books, 2006), 104.

Lesson 4—Loved as God's Daughter

1. J.I. Packer, *Knowing God* (Downers Grove, IL: InterVarsity Press, 1973), 182.
2. John MacArthur, *The MacArthur New Testament Commentary: Romans 1-8* (Chicago, IL: Moody Press, 1991), 13.
3. Vine, et al., *Vine's Complete Expository Dictionary of Old and New Testament Words*, 143.
4. Beth Moore, *Breaking Free: Making Liberty in Christ a Reality in Life* (Nashville, TN: Thomas Nelson Publishers, 1985), 160.

Lesson 5—Valued in Jesus' Teaching

1. Erwin Lutzer and Rebecca Lutzer, *Jesus, Lover of a Woman's Soul* (Carol Stream, IL: Tyndale House Publishers, Inc., 2006), 10.

2. Ibid., 11.

3. *Reflections of Hope Bible Study* (Colorado Springs, CO: International Bible Society, 2009), 17.

4. Diane Dempsey Matt, *The Reluctant Traveler* (Colorado Springs, CO: NavPress Publishing Group, 2002), 155.

Lesson 6—Restored Through Jesus' Ministry

1. Max Lucado, *Come Thirsty* (Nashville, TN: Thomas Nelson, 2007), 22.

2. www.unmarried.org/statistics.html.

3. Mark Rutland, *Streams of Mercy* (Ann Arbor, MI: Servant Publications, 1999), 39,40.

4. Nancy Leigh DeMoss, *Brokenness: The Heart God Revives* (Chicago, IL: Moody Publishers, 2002), 54-55.

Lesson 8—Invited into Jesus' Classroom

1. Peter Kreeft, *Three Philosophies of Life* (San Francisco, CA: Ignarius Press, 1989), 99.

2. Martyn Lloyd-Jones, *Spiritual Depression* (Grand Rapids, MI: William B. Eerdmans, 1965), 21.

3. Kenneth L. Barker and John R. Kohlenberger III, *NIV Commentary, Volume I: Old Testament* (Grand Rapids, MI: Zondervan Publishing House, 1994), 292.

Lesson 9—Affirmed in God's Family

1. John MacArthur, *The MacArthur Bible Commentary* (Nashville, TN: Thomas Nelson, Inc., 2005), 1154.

2. Ibid.

3. Carolyn Custis James, *The Gospel of Ruth* (Grand Rapids, MI: Zondervan Publishing House, 2006), 66.

Lesson 10—Called out of the Shadows

1. Ken Gire, *The Reflective Life* (Colorado Springs, CO: Chariot Victor Publishing, 1998), 23.

2. William D. Mounce, *Mounce's Complete Expository Dictionary of Old and New Testament Words* (Grand Rapids, MI: Zondervan Publishing House, 2006), 128.

Lesson 12—Empowered by the Holy Spirit

1. Kenneth S. Kantzer, "Proceed with Care," *Christianity Today*, October 3, 1986.

2. Rick Warren, *The Purpose Driven® Life* (Grand Rapids, MI: Zondervan Publishing House, 2002), 230.

Lesson 13—Chosen for Such a Time as This

1. Michael Richardson, *Amazing Faith: The Authorized Biography of Bill Bright* (Colorado Springs, CO: Waterbrook Press, 2000), 76.

2. Victory C. Pfitzner, *Paul and the Agon Motif: Traditional Athletic Imagery in the Pauline Literature* (Leiden, Netherlands: Brill, 1967), 120.

3. Warren, *The Purpose Driven® Life*, 23.

About the Author

Sharon Jaynes is an international inspirational speaker and Bible teacher for women's conferences and events. She is the author of several books, including *Becoming the Woman of His Dreams, The Power of a Woman's Words, Your Scars Are Beautiful to God, Becoming Spiritually Beautiful, "I'm Not Good Enough"...and Other Lies Women Tell Themselves,* and *Becoming a Woman Who Listens to God.* Her books have been translated into several foreign languages and impact women around the globe. Her passion is to encourage, equip, and empower women to walk in courage and confidence as they grasp their true identity as a child of God and a co-heir with Christ.

Sharon is a cofounder of Girlfriends in God, a conference and online ministry that crosses denominational, racial, and generational boundaries to unify the body of Christ. To learn more, visit www.girlfriendsinGod.com.

Sharon and her husband, Steve, have one grown son, Steven. They call North Carolina home.

Sharon is always honored to hear from her readers. You can contact her directly at Sharon@sharonjaynes.com or at her mailing address:

Sharon Jaynes
PO Box 725
Matthews, NC 28106

To learn more about Sharon's books and speaking ministry or to inquire about having her speak at your next event, visit www.sharonjaynes.com.